ELEANOR

Higher
Maths

PAST PAPER SOLUTIONS
2011/12 Edition

Steven O'Hagan
George Kinnear

Higher Still Notes

ISBN: 978 0 9557067 4 5

Published by Higher Still Notes
www.hsn.uk.net

Note: The contents of this book have not been checked or approved by the Scottish Qualifications Authority. They reflect the authors' opinion of good answers to exam questions and have been checked against publicly available marking instructions.

Printed by Bell & Bain Ltd., Glasgow, Scotland, UK.

Contents

Introduction

How to use this book

Past papers are probably the best practice you can get for the actual exam, so you should plan to do as many as possible. Make sure you practice doing a whole paper in the allocated time, so you can get used to the pace.

The best way to use this book is for checking your answers *after* you have tried the questions yourself. Don't just read the solutions whenever you get stuck!

Here are some features of the book which should help you:

Questions and parts

The question number is shown in the big circle, making it easy to spot at a glance.

All the parts of the question, including subparts, are also labelled.

References to notes

The grey box at the start of each solution has pointers to useful sections of our free Higher Maths notes (see below for details).

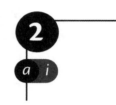

The "§" symbol just means "section", so the example to the right says you should look up Section 3 in the notes for Integration.

Clouds

You'll notice these in a lot of solutions.

They usually contain helpful reminders, or explanations of the steps in the working.

Get more help with Higher Maths

You can download a free set of Higher Maths notes on our website:

www.hsn.uk.net/Higher-Maths

and you can also join our online forum, where you can chat with other students and ask about any questions you're stuck on:

www.hsn.uk.net/forum

	2007 P1	2007 P2	SQP 1 P1	SQP 1 P2	2008 P1	2008 P2	SQP 2 P1	SQP 2 P2	2009 P1	2009 P2	2010 P1	2010 P2	2011 P1	2011 P2
Straight Lines	1			1	7	1	1, 3, 11		3, 5, 15, 21		1, 21a,b	5a	2, 8, 21	5a
Functions and Graphs	3	4a	2, 6, 17		8, 17, 19, 20, 23a	3a	14		10, 14, 23	2a, 5a	4, 11, 20		3, 20	2a,b
Differentiation	9	5a, 6	1, 22	4a, 5b	21a,c, 22	6	12, 21	3, 5, 7	4, 8, 20	1, 2b	12, 15, 17	5b	4, 22	
Sequences	7		5, 21		1, 4		2, 8		1, 6		2, 7			3
Polynomials and Quadratics	4, 8a,b	5b, 10a	7, 12, 14, 23		10, 13, 16, 21b		4, 5, 7, 17	2	12, 19	3a	5, 6, 13, 16, 18, 22		5, 7, 9, 17, 18	2c,d
Integration	8c	10b	3, 13	5a		7	20, 25	9	16	5c	14	6c	11, 16	4
Trigonometry	6	2, 4b	8, 9, 24	7	6, 9	5	9, 23, 24		7, 11, 24	5b	23	4	10, 12, 23	6b
Circles	5	3, 5c	10, 15	4b	2, 5	4		6	2, 9	4	8	3	6	7
Vectors	2	1	4, 11, 18	2, 4c	3, 11, 12, 18	2	10, 15, 16	1	17, 22	7	3, 10, 21c	1	1, 14, 15	1
Further Calculus	10	7	16		14, 15	3c	6, 18, 19		18		9	6a	13	6b
Exponentials and Logarithms		8, 9, 11	19, 20	6	23b		13, 22	8	10	3b, 6	19	7	19	5
Wave Functions	11			3		3b		4	13			2		6a

5

Formulae List

Circle

The equation $x^2 + y^2 + 2gx + 2fy + c = 0$ represents a circle centre $(-g, -f)$ and radius $\sqrt{g^2 + f^2 - c}$.

The equation $(x - a)^2 + (y - b)^2 = r^2$ represents a circle centre (a, b) and radius r.

Scalar Product

$$\mathbf{a.b} = |\mathbf{a}||\mathbf{b}|\cos\theta \text{ where } \theta \text{ is the angle between } \mathbf{a} \text{ and } \mathbf{b}.$$

or $\quad \mathbf{a.b} = a_1 b_1 + a_2 b_2 + a_3 b_3$ where $\mathbf{a} = \begin{pmatrix} a_1 \\ a_2 \\ a_3 \end{pmatrix}$ and $\mathbf{b} = \begin{pmatrix} b_1 \\ b_2 \\ b_3 \end{pmatrix}$.

Trigonometric formulae

$$\sin(A \pm B) = \sin A \cos B \pm \cos A \sin B$$
$$\cos(A \pm B) = \cos A \cos B \mp \sin A \sin B$$
$$\sin 2A = 2 \sin A \cos A$$
$$\cos 2A = \cos^2 A - \sin^2 A$$
$$= 2\cos^2 A - 1$$
$$= 1 - 2\sin^2 A$$

Table of standard derivatives

$f(x)$	$f'(x)$
$\sin ax$	$a \cos ax$
$\cos ax$	$-a \sin ax$

Table of standard integrals

$f(x)$	$\int f(x)\, dx$
$\sin ax$	$-\frac{1}{a} \cos ax + c$
$\cos ax$	$\frac{1}{a} \sin ax + c$

1

See **Straight Lines** §3 and §6

Method 1

$$3x - y + 2 = 0$$
$$y = 3x + 2$$
$$\text{So } m = 3.$$

Remember:
To extract the gradient, rearrange to the form $y = mx + c$.

Any line parallel to this has gradient 3.

The equation is $y - 4 = 3(x - (-1))$ using point $(-1, 4)$
$$y - 4 = 3x + 3$$
$$3x - y + 7 = 0.$$

Method 2 The equation of the line has the form
$3x - y + c = 0$ and passes through $(-1, 4)$.

So $3(-1) - 4 + c = 0$
$$-7 + c = 0$$
$$c = 7.$$

So the line has equation $3x - y + 7 = 0$.

2

See **Vectors** §10

$$\overrightarrow{BC} = 2\overrightarrow{AB}$$
$$\underline{c} - \underline{b} = 2(\underline{b} - \underline{a})$$
$$\underline{c} = 2\underline{b} - 2\underline{a} + \underline{b}$$
$$= 3\underline{b} - 2\underline{a}$$

Remember:
$\overrightarrow{AB} = \underline{b} - \underline{a}$

$$= 3\begin{pmatrix} 1 \\ 3 \\ 2 \end{pmatrix} - 2\begin{pmatrix} -2 \\ 1 \\ -1 \end{pmatrix}$$

$$= \begin{pmatrix} 3 \\ 9 \\ 6 \end{pmatrix} - \begin{pmatrix} -4 \\ 2 \\ -2 \end{pmatrix}$$

$$= \begin{pmatrix} 7 \\ 7 \\ 8 \end{pmatrix}. \quad \text{So C is the point } (7, 7, 8).$$

3

See **Functions and Graphs** §3

a) $g(f(x)) = g(x^2+1) = 1-2(x^2+1) = 1-2x^2-2 = -1-2x^2.$

b) $g(g(x)) = g(1-2x) = 1-2(1-2x) = 1-2+4x = 4x-1.$

4

See **Polynomials and Quadratics** §2

For no real roots, $b^2-4ac < 0$ where $a=k, b=-1, c=-1$

$$(-1)^2 - 4k(-1) < 0$$
$$1 + 4k < 0$$
$$4k < -1$$
$$k < -\frac{1}{4}.$$

5

See **Circles** §3 and §1

Large circle centred at B: $x^2 + y^2 - 14x - 16y + 77 = 0$

$$2g = -14 \qquad 2f = -16 \qquad c = 77.$$
$$g = -7 \qquad f = -8$$

Centre: $(-g, -f) = (7, 8).$

Radius: $\sqrt{g^2+f^2-c} = \sqrt{49+64-77} = \sqrt{36} = 6$ units.

So each small circle has radius $\frac{6}{3} = 2$ units.

Let D have coordinates $(x, 8)$. Then since each small circle has radius 2, $x = 7 + 4 \times 2 = 15$. So D is $(15, 8)$.

The x-coord. of B.   4 small radii.

The circle centred at D has equation
$$(x-15)^2 + (y-8)^2 = 4.$$

6

See **Trigonometry** §5

$$\sin 2x° = 6\cos x°$$
$$2\sin x°\cos x° = 6\cos x°$$
$$2\sin x°\cos x° - 6\cos x° = 0$$
$$2\cos x°\left(\sin x° - 3\right) = 0$$
$$\cos x°\left(\sin x° - 3\right) = 0$$

$$\cos x° = 0 \qquad \text{or} \qquad \sin x° - 3 = 0$$
$$x = 90, 270. \qquad\qquad \sin x° = 3$$

No solutions
since $-1 \leqslant \sin x° \leqslant 1$.

So $x = 90, 270$.

7

See **Sequences** – (a) §1 and §2, (b) §4

a $u_1 = \frac{1}{4}u_0 + 16 = \frac{1}{4} \times 0 + 16 = 16$.

$u_2 = \frac{1}{4}u_1 + 16 = \frac{1}{4} \times 16 + 16 = 4 + 16 = 20$.

$u_3 = \frac{1}{4} \times u_2 + 16 = \frac{1}{4} \times 20 + 16 = 5 + 16 = 21$.

b **i** The sequence has a limit because $-1 < \frac{1}{4} < 1$.

ii **Method 1** $k = \frac{b}{1-a}$ where $a = \frac{1}{4}$ and $b = 16$.

$$k = \frac{16}{1 - 1/4} = \frac{16}{3/4} = \frac{4}{3} \times 16 = \frac{64}{3}.$$

Method 2 As $n \to \infty$, $u_{n+1} = u_n = k$. So

$$k = \frac{1}{4}k + 16$$
$$\frac{3}{4}k = 16$$
$$k = \frac{4}{3} \times 16$$
$$= \frac{64}{3}$$

8

(a) and (b) See **Polynomials and Quadratics** §9
(c) See **Integration** §5

a Evaluate y when $x = 3 \ldots$

$$
\begin{array}{r|rrrr}
3 & 1 & -4 & 1 & 6 \\
  &   & 3 & -3 & -6 \\
\hline
  & 1 & -1 & -2 & \boxed{0}
\end{array}
$$

OR

$$y = 3^3 - 4 \times 3^2 + 3 + 6$$
$$= 27 - 36 + 9$$
$$= 0.$$

So the curve crosses the x-axis at $(3, 0)$.

b Since $x = 3$ is a root, $(x-3)$ is a factor.

So $x^3 - 4x^2 + x + 6 = (x-3)(x^2 - x - 2)$
$$= (x-3)(x+1)(x-2).$$

> Either from the bottom row of the table or by inspection.

So A has coordinates $(2, 0)$.

c The shaded area is

$$\int_0^2 (x^3 - 4x^2 + x + 6)\, dx = \left[\frac{x^4}{4} - \frac{4x^3}{3} + \frac{x^2}{2} + 6x \right]_0^2$$
$$= \frac{2^4}{4} - \frac{4 \times 2^3}{3} + \frac{2^2}{2} + 6 \times 2$$
$$= 4 - \frac{32}{3} + 2 + 12$$
$$= 18 - 10\tfrac{2}{3}$$
$$= 7\tfrac{1}{3} \text{ square units}$$
$$\left(\text{or } \frac{22}{3} \text{ square units.} \right)$$

9

*See **Differentiation** §7, §8 and §9*

a When $x = 0$, $f(0) = 3 \times 0 - 0^3 = 0$.

When $y = 0$, $3x - x^3 = 0$

$$x(3 - x^2) = 0$$

$$x = 0 \qquad \text{or} \qquad 3 - x^2 = 0$$

$$x = \pm\sqrt{3}.$$

So the curve passes through $(-\sqrt{3}, 0)$, $(0, 0)$ and $(\sqrt{3}, 0)$.

b Stationary points exist where $f'(x) = 0$.

$$f'(x) = 3 - 3x^2 = 0$$

$$x^2 = 1$$

$$x = \pm 1.$$

When $x = 1$, $y = 3 \times 1 - 1^3 = 3 - 1 = 2$. $\qquad (1, 2)$

When $x = -1$, $y = 3 \times (-1) - (-1)^3 = -3 + 1 = -2$. $(-1, -2)$.

Method 1 Nature table...

x	-1^-	-1	-1^+	1^-	1	1^+
$f'(x)$	$-$	0	$+$	$+$	0	$-$
Sketch	$\searrow$	$-$	$\nearrow$	$\nearrow$	$-$	$\searrow$

Method 2 The second derivative test... $f''(x) = -6x$.

$$f(-1) > 0, \quad f(1) < 0.$$

So $(-1, -2)$ is a minimum turning point and

$(1, 2)$ is a maximum turning point.

c

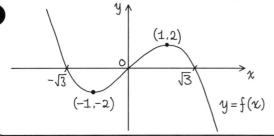

10

See **Further Calculus** §4

$$y = (3x^2+2)^{1/2}$$
$$\frac{dy}{dx} = \frac{1}{2}(3x^2+2)^{-1/2} \times \frac{d}{dx}(3x^2+2)$$
$$= \frac{1}{2}(3x^2+2)^{-1/2} \times 6x$$
$$= \frac{3x}{\sqrt{3x^2+2}}.$$

Remember the Chain Rule

11

See **Wave Functions** §6

a

$$\sqrt{3}\cos x + \sin x = k\cos(x-a)$$
$$= k\cos x \cos a + k\sin x \sin a$$
$$= (k\cos a)\cos x + (k\sin a)\sin x$$

Comparing coefficients: $k\sin a = 1$ $k\cos a = \sqrt{3}$

$\begin{array}{c|c} \checkmark \; S & A \; \checkmark\checkmark \\ \hline T & C \; \checkmark \end{array}$

So $k = \sqrt{1^2 + \sqrt{3}^2}$ and $\tan a = \frac{k\sin a}{k\cos a} = \frac{1}{\sqrt{3}}$.
$$= \sqrt{4}$$
$$= 2$$
$$a = \frac{\pi}{6}.$$

Exact value...

So $\sqrt{3}\cos x + \sin x = 2\cos\left(x - \frac{\pi}{6}\right)$.

b

- The amplitude is 2.
- This is the graph of $y = 2\cos x$ shifted $\frac{\pi}{6}$ to the right.
- When $x = 0$, $y = 2\cos\left(-\frac{\pi}{6}\right) = \sqrt{3}$

2007 Paper 2

1

See **Vectors** §7 and §12

a $G(0,2,2)$.

b From the diagram

$$p = \tfrac{1}{2}g = \tfrac{1}{2}\begin{pmatrix} 0 \\ 2 \\ 2 \end{pmatrix} = \begin{pmatrix} 0 \\ 1 \\ 1 \end{pmatrix}.$$

$$q = \underline{b} + \tfrac{1}{2}\overrightarrow{BG} = \underline{b} + \tfrac{1}{2}(g - \underline{b}) = \tfrac{1}{2}(\underline{b} + g) = \tfrac{1}{2}\begin{pmatrix} 2 \\ 4 \\ 2 \end{pmatrix} = \begin{pmatrix} 1 \\ 2 \\ 1 \end{pmatrix}.$$

c $|p| = \sqrt{1^2 + 1^2} = \sqrt{2}$, $|q| = \sqrt{1^2 + 2^2 + 1^2} = \sqrt{6}$.

$$p \cdot q = 0 \times 1 + 1 \times 2 + 1 \times 1 = 3$$

So $\cos P\hat{O}Q = \dfrac{p \cdot q}{|p||q|}$

Using:
$\underline{a} \cdot \underline{b} = |\underline{a}||\underline{b}|\cos\theta$

$$= \frac{3}{\sqrt{2}\sqrt{6}}$$

$$= \frac{3}{2\sqrt{3}}$$

$$= \frac{\sqrt{3}}{2}$$

Exact value...

$$P\hat{O}Q = \cos^{-1}\left(\frac{\sqrt{3}}{2}\right) = 30° \quad \left(\text{or } \frac{\pi}{6} \text{ radians}\right)$$

2

See **Trigonometry** – (a) §3, (b) §4

Using Pythagoras's Theorem...

$\sin c = \dfrac{1}{\sqrt{5}}$ $\cos c = \dfrac{2}{\sqrt{5}}$

$\sin d = \dfrac{1}{\sqrt{10}}$ $\cos d = \dfrac{3}{\sqrt{10}}$

cont...

a $\sin(c+d) = \sin c \cdot \cos d + \cos c \sin d$

$$= \frac{1}{\sqrt{5}} \times \frac{3}{\sqrt{10}} + \frac{2}{\sqrt{5}} \times \frac{1}{\sqrt{10}}$$

$$= \frac{3+2}{\sqrt{5}\sqrt{10}}$$

$$= \frac{5}{5\sqrt{2}}$$

$$= \frac{1}{\sqrt{2}}$$

b **i** $\sin 2c = 2\sin c \cos c = 2 \times \frac{1}{\sqrt{5}} \times \frac{2}{\sqrt{5}} = \frac{4}{5}$.

ii $\cos 2d = 2\cos^2 d - 1$

$$= 2 \times \frac{9}{10} - 1$$

> Any of the three formulae for cos2d could be used here.

$$= \frac{9}{5} - \frac{5}{5}$$

$$= \frac{4}{5}.$$

3

See **Circles** §4

To find points of intersection, put $y = 6 - 2x$ into the equation of the circle:

$$x^2 + (6-2x)^2 + 6x - 4(6-2x) - 7 = 0$$

$$x^2 + 36 - 24x + 4x^2 + 6x - 24 + 8x - 7 = 0$$

$$5x^2 - 10x + 5 = 0$$

$$x^2 - 2x + 1 = 0$$

> You could also use the discriminant to show there is just one solution.

$$(x-1)^2 = 0$$

$$x = 1$$

Since there is only one solution, the line is a tangent to the circle.

When $x = 1$, $y = 6 - 2 \times 1 = 4$.

So the point of contact is $(1, 4)$.

4

(a) See **Functions and Graphs** §9 and §10
(b) See **Trigonometry** §1

a The amplitude is 2, so $a = 2$.

There are three complete waves in 360° so $b = 3$.

The graph is the same as $y = a\sin(bx°)$ but shifted down 1.

So $c = -1$.

b $2\sin(3x°) - 1 = 0$

$\quad\quad \sin(3x°) = \frac{1}{2}$

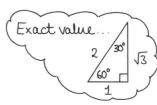

$3x = 30 \quad$ or $\quad 180 - 30$

$3x = 30 \quad$ or $\quad 150$

$x = 10 \quad$ or $\quad 50$

From the diagram, the x-coordinate of P is 50.

5

(a) See **Differentiation** §5 or **Polynomials and Quadratics** §7
(b) See **Polynomials and Quadratics** §7
(c) See **Circles** §6

a <u>Method 1</u> $\quad \frac{dy}{dx} = 2 \times \frac{1}{2}x - 8 = x - 8.$

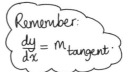

$m_{tangent} = 4$ i.e. $\frac{dy}{dx} = 4$

So $x - 8 = 4$

$\quad\quad x = 12.$

When $x = 12$, $y = \frac{1}{2} \times 12^2 - 8 \times 12 + 34 = 72 - 96 + 34 = 10$

So Q is the point $(12, 10)$.

cont...

Method 2 The tangent has the form $y = 4x + c$. There is just one point of intersection with the parabola.

So $\frac{1}{2}x^2 - 8x + 34 = 4x + c$

$\frac{1}{2}x^2 - 12x + 34 - c = 0$ has discriminant zero.

So $x = -\frac{b}{2a}$ where $a = \frac{1}{2}$, $b = -12$

$= \frac{12}{2 \times \frac{1}{2}} = 12.$

> From the quadratic formula:
> $x = \frac{-b \pm \sqrt{b^2 - 4ac}}{2a}$

When $x = 12$, $y = \frac{1}{2} \times 12^2 - 8 \times 12 + 34 = 72 - 96 + 34 = 10.$

So Q is the point $(12, 10)$.

b P has the same y-coordinate as Q, so

$\frac{1}{2}x^2 - 8x + 34 = 10$ ← The y-coord. of P.

$\frac{1}{2}x^2 - 8x - 24 = 0$

$x^2 - 16x - 48 = 0$ multiplying through by 2.

$(x - 4)(x - 12) = 0$

$x = 4$ or $x = 12.$

So P is the point $(4, 10)$.

c C has x-coordinate 8 by symmetry.

Let C be the point $(8, y)$.

$m_{CQ} \times m_{tgt.} = -1$ since CQ is a radius.

So $m_{CQ} = -\frac{1}{4}$. However, $m_{CQ} = \frac{10 - y}{12 - 8} = \frac{10 - y}{4}.$

So $\frac{10 - y}{4} = -\frac{1}{4}$

$10 - y = -1$

$y = 11.$

So C is the point $(8, 11)$.

6

See **Differentiation** §12 or **Polynomials and Quadratics** §3 and §1

a **i** Using Pythagoras's Theorem: $ST = \sqrt{10^2 + 10^2} = \sqrt{200} = 10\sqrt{2}$.

ii

$\bullet = 45°$ since the large triangle is isosceles.

$* = 45°$ since the angles in a triangle and on a straight line sum to $180°$.

So the shaded area is $A = $ length $\times$ breadth

$$= (10\sqrt{2} - 2x)x$$

$$= 10\sqrt{2}\,x - 2x^2 \text{ square metres}$$

b **Method 1**   Stationary points exist where $\frac{dA}{dx} = 0$.

$$\frac{dA}{dx} = 10\sqrt{2} - 4x = 0$$

$$4x = 10\sqrt{2}$$

$$x = \frac{10\sqrt{2}}{4}$$

$$= \frac{5\sqrt{2}}{2}.$$

Nature...

x	$\frac{5\sqrt{2}}{2}^-$	$\frac{5\sqrt{2}}{2}$	$\frac{5\sqrt{2}}{2}^+$
$\frac{dA}{dx}$	$+$	0	$-$
Sketch	/	—	\

or $\frac{d^2A}{dx^2} = -4$.

Hence $x = \frac{5\sqrt{2}}{2}$ gives the maximum area.

cont...

Method 2 Completing the square...

$$A = -2x^2 + 10\sqrt{2}\,x$$

$$= -2\left(x^2 - 5\sqrt{2}\,x\right)$$

$$= -2\left(x - \frac{5\sqrt{2}}{2}\right)^2 + 2\left(\frac{5\sqrt{2}}{2}\right)^2$$

The x-coordinate of the turning point is $x = \frac{5\sqrt{2}}{2}$.

The turning point is a maximum since the x^2-coefficient is negative.

Hence $x = \frac{5\sqrt{2}}{2}$ gives the maximum area.

When the breadth is $\frac{5\sqrt{2}}{2}$ metres, the length is

$$10\sqrt{2} - 2 \times \frac{5\sqrt{2}}{2} = 5\sqrt{2} \text{ metres.}$$

7

*See **Further Calculus** §6*

$$\int_0^2 \sin(4x+1)\,dx$$

$$= \left[-\tfrac{1}{4}\cos(4x+1)\right]_0^2$$

Using
$$\int \sin ax\,dx = -\tfrac{1}{a}\cos ax + c.$$

$$= -\tfrac{1}{4}\cos(4 \times 2 + 1) + \tfrac{1}{4}\cos(4 \times 0 + 1)$$

$$= -\tfrac{1}{4}\cos 9 + \tfrac{1}{4}\cos 1$$

$$= 0.363 \quad \text{(to 3 d.p.)}$$

Remember: We must work in radians when doing calculus.

8

See **Exponentials and Logarithms** §5

Put $x = a$ and $y = 0$ into the equation:

$$0 = \log_3 (a-1) - 2 \cdot 2$$
$$\log_3(a-1) = 2 \cdot 2$$
$$a - 1 = 3^{2 \cdot 2}$$
$$a = 3^{2 \cdot 2} + 1$$
$$= 12 \cdot 212 \quad \text{(to 3 d.p.)}$$

Remember:
$$x = \log_a y \Leftrightarrow a^x = y$$

9

See **Exponentials and Logarithms** §7

a $y = a^{-x}$. Reflect in the y-axis.

b $y = a^{1-x} = a \times a^{-x}$. The graph is as above but scaled by a in the y-direction — each y-coordinate is multiplied by $a > 0$.

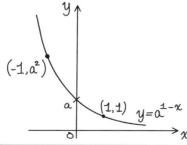

Also, when $x = 1$,
$$y = a^{1-1} = a^0 = 1.$$

So the curve passes through the point $(1, 1)$.

10

(a) See **Polynomials and Quadratics** §5
(b) See **Integration** §3

a **i** The curve $y = f'(x)$ has roots $x = 2$ and $x = 4$. So $x-2$ and $x-4$ are factors of $f'(x)$.
So $a = 2$ and $b = 4$ (or vice versa).

ii We know that $f'(0) = 6$, so

$$k(0-4)(0-2) = 6$$
$$8k = 6$$
$$k = \frac{6}{8}$$
$$= \frac{3}{4}.$$

b $f(x) = \int f'(x)\, dx$

$$= \frac{3}{4} \int (x-2)(x-4)\, dx$$
$$= \frac{3}{4} \int (x^2 - 6x + 8)\, dx$$
$$= \frac{3}{4} \left(\frac{x^3}{3} - 3x^2 + 8x \right) + c$$

From the question, $f(0) = 6$. So $c = 6$. Therefore:
$$f(x) = \frac{3}{4} \left(\frac{x^3}{3} - 3x^2 + 8x \right) + 6 = \frac{1}{4}x^3 - \frac{9}{4}x^2 + 6x + 6.$$

11

See **Exponentials and Logarithms** – (a) and (b) §5, (c) §6

a Put $x = a$ and $y = 6$ in the equation:

$$6 = 3 \times 4^a$$
$$4^a = 2$$
$$a = \frac{1}{2} \text{ since } 4^{1/2} = \sqrt{4} = 2.$$

cont...

b Put $x = -\frac{1}{2}$ and $y = b$ in the equation:

$b = 3 \times 4^{-\frac{1}{2}}$

$= \dfrac{3}{\sqrt{4}}$

$= \dfrac{3}{2}$.

Remember:
$u^{-m} = \dfrac{1}{u^m}$.

c <u>Method 1</u> $y = 3 \times 4^x$

$\log_{10} y = \log_{10}(3 \times 4^x)$ taking $\log_{10}$ on both sides

$= \log_{10} 3 + \log_{10} 4^x$

$= \log_{10} 3 + x \log_{10} 4$

Remember:
- $\log_a xy = \log_a x + \log_a y$.
- $k \log_a x = \log_a x^k$

So $\log_{10} y = (\log_{10} 4) x + \log_{10} 3$

The gradient is $\log_{10} 4$. (Comparing to $y = mx + c$.)

<u>Method 2</u>   Start with $\log_{10} y = Px + Q$ and find P and Q.

$\log_{10} y = Px + Q$

$y = 10^{Px + Q}$

$y = 10^Q \times 10^{Px}$

Comparing to $y = 3 \times 4^x$ ...

$10^Q = 3$ and $10^{Px} = 4^x$

$Q = \log_{10} 3$ $(10^P)^x = 4^x$

$10^P = 4$

$P = \log_{10} 4$.

The gradient is $P = \log_{10} 4$.

SQP 1 Paper 1

1

See **Differentiation** §2

$$y = \frac{x^3 - x}{x^2} = \frac{x^3}{x^2} - \frac{x}{x^2} = x - x^{-1}.$$

$$\frac{dy}{dx} = 1 + x^{-2} = 1 + \frac{1}{x^2}.$$

Remember:
$$\frac{x^a}{x^b} = x^{a-b}.$$

B

2

See **Functions and Graphs** §3

$$g(f(x)) = g(2x-3) = (2x-3)^2 = 4x^2 - 12x + 9.$$

A

3

See **Integration** §1 and §2

$$\int \frac{1}{3\sqrt{x}}\, dx = \int x^{-1/3}\, dx$$

$$= \frac{x^{2/3}}{2/3} + C$$

$$= \frac{3}{2} x^{2/3} + C$$

Remember:
$$\frac{a}{b/c} = a \times \frac{c}{b}$$

C

4

See **Vectors** §3

$$d_{AB}^2 = \left(2 - (-1)\right)^2 + \left(3 - (-4)\right)^2 + \left(-2 - 0\right)^2$$

$$= 3^2 + 7^2 + (-2)^2$$

$$= 9 + 49 + 4$$

$$= 62.$$

So $d_{AB} = \sqrt{62}$.

C

5

See **Sequences** §1 and §2

$u_0 = -1$

$u_1 = 3u_0 - 4 = 3 \times (-1) - 4 = -3 - 4 = -7.$

$u_2 = 3u_1 - 4 = 3 \times (-7) - 4 = -21 - 4 = -25.$

A

6

See **Functions and Graphs** §10

$y = -3 - f(x) = -f(x) - 3.$

Reflect in x-axis → Shift down 3 →

$y=f(x)$ $y=-f(x)$ $y=-f(x)-3$

A

7

See **Polynomials and Quadratics** §3 and §1

The turning point is $(4, -5)$.
Since the x^2 coefficient is $3 > 0$,
the parabola is concave up, i.e.
$\cup$-shaped.
So the turning point is a minimum.

Remember:
The parabola $y = a(x-p)^2 + q$ has turning point (p, q).

C

8

See **Trigonometry** §4

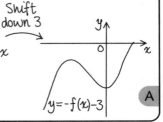

$\sin 2x° = 2\sin x° \cos x°$

$\qquad = 2 \times \dfrac{2\sqrt{2}}{3} \times \dfrac{1}{3}$

$\qquad = \dfrac{4\sqrt{2}}{9}$

$\sin x° = \dfrac{\text{opposite}}{\text{hypotenuse}} = \dfrac{2\sqrt{2}}{3}.$

$\cos x° = \dfrac{\text{adjacent}}{\text{hypotenuse}} = \dfrac{1}{3}.$

A

9

See **Trigonometry** §3

$$\sin(a-b) = \sin a \cos b - \cos a \sin b$$
$$= \frac{1}{\sqrt{5}} \times \frac{4}{\sqrt{17}} - \frac{2}{\sqrt{5}} \times \frac{1}{\sqrt{17}}$$
$$= \frac{4-2}{\sqrt{5}\sqrt{17}}$$
$$= \frac{2}{\sqrt{85}}$$

Remember: $\sqrt{x}\sqrt{y} = \sqrt{xy}$

$$\sin a = \frac{\text{opp.}}{\text{hyp.}} = \frac{1}{\sqrt{5}}$$

$$\cos a = \frac{\text{adj.}}{\text{hyp.}} = \frac{2}{\sqrt{5}}$$

$$\sin b = \frac{1}{\sqrt{17}}, \quad \cos b = \frac{4}{\sqrt{17}}$$

B

10

See **Circles** §3

The radius is $\sqrt{g^2 + f^2 - c}$ where $g = 4$, $f = -3$ and $c = -12$.

i.e. $\sqrt{4^2 + (-3)^2 - (-12)} = \sqrt{16 + 9 + 12} = \sqrt{37}$.

C

11

See **Vectors** §9

Since points P, Q and R are collinear, $\vec{QR} = k\vec{PQ}$ for some constant k.

$$\vec{PQ} = q - p = \begin{pmatrix} 5 \\ 13 \\ 13 \end{pmatrix} - \begin{pmatrix} 1 \\ 3 \\ 7 \end{pmatrix} = \begin{pmatrix} 4 \\ 10 \\ 6 \end{pmatrix}$$

$$\vec{QR} = r - q = \begin{pmatrix} s \\ 33 \\ 25 \end{pmatrix} - \begin{pmatrix} 5 \\ 13 \\ 13 \end{pmatrix} = \begin{pmatrix} s-5 \\ 20 \\ 12 \end{pmatrix}$$

So each component of $\vec{QR}$ is twice the component of $\vec{PQ}$

So
$$s - 5 = 2 \times 4$$
$$s = 8 + 5$$
$$s = 13.$$

C

SQP 1

SQP 1

12

See **Polynomials and Quadratics** §3

<u>Method 1</u>

$$2x^2 - 12x + 11 = 2(x^2 - 6x) + 11$$
$$= 2(x-3)^2 - 18 + 11$$
$$= 2(x-3)^2 - 7. \text{ So } c = -7.$$

<u>Method 2</u> Comparing coefficients...

$$2x^2 - 12x + 11 = 2(x-b)^2 + c$$
$$= 2(x^2 - 2bx + b^2) + c$$
$$= 2x^2 - 4bx + 2b^2 + c.$$

So $4b = 12$ and $2b^2 + c = 11$
$$b = 3.$$
$$c = 11 - 2 \times 3^2$$
$$c = 11 - 18$$
$$c = -7.$$

B

13

See **Integration** §3

$$y = \int \frac{dy}{dx}\, dx$$
$$= \int (3x^2 + 9x + 1)\, dx$$
$$= \frac{3x^3}{3} + \frac{9x^2}{2} + x + c$$
$$= x^3 + \frac{9}{2}x^2 + x + c.$$

The curve passes through the origin, so $y = 0$ when $x = 0$.
Hence $c = 0$ and so $y = x^3 + \frac{9}{2}x^2 + x.$

A

14

See **Polynomials and Quadratics** §2

For equal roots, $b^2 - 4ac = 0$ where $a = 1$, $b = -3$ and $c = k$.

$$(-3)^2 - 4 \times 1 \times k = 0$$
$$9 - 4k = 0$$
$$k = \frac{9}{4}.$$

D

15

See **Circles** §6

The centre of the circle is $(3, 4)$.

So $m_{radius} = \dfrac{4-2}{3-(-1)} = \dfrac{2}{4} = \dfrac{1}{2}$

$\therefore m_{tgt} = -2$ since the radius and tangent are perpendicular.

A

16

See **Further Calculus** §6

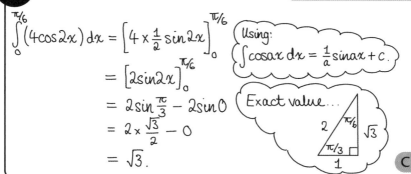

$$\int_0^{\pi/6} (4\cos 2x)\, dx = \left[4 \times \frac{1}{2}\sin 2x \right]_0^{\pi/6}$$

Using:
$$\int \cos ax\, dx = \frac{1}{a}\sin ax + c.$$

$$= \left[2\sin 2x \right]_0^{\pi/6}$$
$$= 2\sin\frac{\pi}{3} - 2\sin 0$$

Exact value...

$$= 2 \times \frac{\sqrt{3}}{2} - 0$$
$$= \sqrt{3}.$$

C

17

See **Functions and Graphs** §9 and §10

There are 2 complete waves in 2π radians, so $p = 2$.
The graph is $y = \sin(2x)$ shifted up 1, so $q = 1$.

A

18

See **Vectors** §11 and §13

The angle ϑ between $\underline{a}$ and $\underline{c}$ is such that $\cos\vartheta = \dfrac{adj.}{hyp.} = \dfrac{3}{5}$.

So $\underline{a}.\underline{c} = |\underline{a}||\underline{c}|\cos\vartheta = 3 \times 5 \times \dfrac{3}{5} = 9$. So (1) is true.

Since $\underline{a}$ and $\underline{b}$ are perpendicular, $\underline{a}.\underline{b} = 0$. So (2) is false. **B**

19

See **Exponentials and Logarithms** §5

__Method 1__

$$\log_3 t - \log_3 5 = 2$$
$$\log_3\left(\frac{t}{5}\right) = 2$$
$$\frac{t}{5} = 3^2$$
$$t = 5 \times 9$$
$$= 45$$

Remember:
• $\log_a x - \log_a y = \log_a \frac{x}{y}$.
• $y = \log_a x \Leftrightarrow x = a^y$.

__Method 2__

$$\log_3 t = 2 + \log_3 5$$
$$= 2\log_3 3 + \log_3 5$$
$$= \log_3 3^2 + \log_3 5$$
$$= \log_3(9 \times 5)$$
$$= \log_3 45$$
$$t = 45.$$

Remember:
• $\log_a a = 1$
• $\log_a x + \log_a y = \log_a xy$
• $\log_a x = \log_a y \Leftrightarrow x = y$

D

20

See **Exponentials and Logarithms** §5

$$3^k = e^4$$
$$\log_e 3^k = \log_e e^4 \qquad \text{taking } \log_e \text{ on both sides}$$
$$k \times \log_e 3 = 4$$
$$k = \frac{4}{\log_e 3}.$$

Remember:
• $\log_a x^k = k\log_a x$
• $\log_a a = 1$

C

21

See **Sequences** §2 and §4

a Product A : $\quad u_{n+1} = 0.3u_n + 300 \qquad u_0 = k$, a constant

$\qquad\qquad$ ↖ 70% of the germs are removed, so 30% remain.

Product B : $\quad v_{n+1} = 0.2v_n + 350 \qquad v_0 = k$.

b As $n \to \infty$, u_n and v_n both tend to limits because

$-1 < 0.3 < 1$ and $-1 < 0.2 < 1$.

<u>Method 1</u> $\quad l_A = \dfrac{300}{1-0.3} = \dfrac{300}{0.7} = \dfrac{3000}{7}$.

$\qquad\qquad l_B = \dfrac{350}{1-0.2} = \dfrac{350}{0.8} = \dfrac{3500}{8}$.

<u>Method 2</u> As $n \to \infty$, $u_{n+1} = u_n = l_A$ and $v_{n+1} = v_n = l_B$.

$\quad l_A = 0.3l_A + 300 \qquad\qquad l_B = 0.2l_B + 350$

$\quad 0.7l_A = 300 \qquad\qquad\quad 0.8l_B = 350$

$\qquad l_A = \dfrac{300}{0.7} \qquad\qquad\qquad l_B = \dfrac{350}{0.8}$

$\qquad\quad = \dfrac{3000}{7} \qquad\qquad\qquad\quad = \dfrac{3500}{8}$

To compare, put over a common denominator:

$\quad l_A = \dfrac{3000}{7} = \dfrac{3000 \times 8}{56} = \dfrac{24\,000}{56}$ ←

$\qquad\qquad\qquad\qquad\qquad\qquad\qquad$ ⎫ So $l_A < l_B$.

$\quad l_B = \dfrac{3500}{8} = \dfrac{3500 \times 7}{56} = \dfrac{24\,500}{56}$ ←

<u>or</u> carry out division:

$\qquad\qquad \dfrac{428.571}{7\overline{)3000.40^50^10}}$ $\quad$ so the number of germs present will settle around 428.

A :

$\qquad\qquad \dfrac{437.5}{8\overline{)3500.30^60^40}}$ $\quad$ so the number of germs present will settle around 437.

B :

So product A is more effective in the long term.

SQP 1

22

See **Differentiation** §7, §8 and §9

a Stationary points exist where $\frac{dy}{dx} = 0$.

$$\frac{dy}{dx} = 3x^2 - 18x + 24 = 0$$
$$x^2 - 6x + 8 = 0 \qquad (\div 3)$$
$$(x-2)(x-4) = 0.$$
$$x - 2 = 0 \quad \text{or} \quad x - 4 = 0$$
$$x = 2 \qquad\qquad x = 4.$$

When $x = 2$, $y = 2^3 - 9 \times 2^2 + 24 \times 2 - 20$
$$= 8 - 36 + 48 - 20$$
$$= 0. \qquad (2, 0)$$

Or use synthetic division.

When $x = 4$, $y = 4^3 - 9 \times 4^2 + 24 \times 4 - 20$
$$= 64 - 9 \times 16 + 96 - 20$$
$$= 140 - 144$$
$$= -4 \qquad (4, -4).$$

Method 1 Nature table:

x	2^-	2	2^+	4^-	4	4^+
$(x-2)$	$-$	0	$+$	$+$		$+$
$(x-4)$	$-$		$-$	$-$	0	$+$
$\frac{dy}{dx}$	$+$	0	$-$	$-$	0	$+$
Sketch	/	―	\	\	_	/

Method 2 Second derivative test: $\frac{d^2y}{dx^2} = 6x - 18$.

When $x = 2$, $\frac{d^2y}{dx^2} = -6 < 0$. When $x = 4$, $\frac{d^2y}{dx^2} = 6 > 0$.

So $(2, 0)$ is a maximum turning point.
$(4, -4)$ is a minimum turning point.

cont...

b i $(x-2)^2(x-5) = (x^2-4x+4)(x-5)$

$\qquad = x^3-4x^2+4x-5x^2+20x-20$

$\qquad = x^3-9x^2+24x-20.$

ii To find the x-axis intercepts, put $y=0$:

$\qquad x^3-9x^2+24x-20 = 0$

$\qquad (x-2)^2(x-5) = 0$

$\qquad x-2=0 \quad$ or $\quad x-5=0$

$\qquad\quad x=2 \qquad\qquad x=5.$

So the curve passes through $(2,0)$ and $(5,0)$.

To find the y-axis intercept, put $x=0$: $\quad y=-20.$
So the curve passes through $(0,-20)$.

Using this information and the stationary points:

SQP 1

23

See **Polynomials and Quadratics** §11 and §9

Equate to find points of intersection...

$\qquad x^3+5x^2-36x+32 = -x^2+x+2$

$\qquad x^3+6x^2-37x+30 = 0.$

cont...

Method 1 By inspection: $(x-1)(x^2+7x-30) = 0$

$$(x-1)(x+10)(x-3) = 0$$

$$x = 1 \text{ or } x = -10 \text{ or } x = 3.$$

Method 2 Evaluate the expression for $x = 1$:

$$\begin{array}{c|cccc} 1 & 1 & 6 & -37 & 30 \\ & & 1 & 7 & -30 \\ \hline & 1 & 7 & -30 & \boxed{0} \end{array}$$

Since the remainder is 0, $x = 1$ is a root so $(x-1)$ is a factor.

$$x^3 + 6x^2 - 37x + 30 = 0$$
$$(x-1)(x^2 + 7x - 30) = 0$$

The coefficients of the other factor come from the bottom row of the table.

$$(x-1)(x+10)(x-3) = 0.$$

$$x = 1 \text{ or } x = -10 \text{ or } x = 3.$$

From the diagram, A has $x = -10$, B has $x = 1$ and C has $x = 3$

24

See **Trigonometry** §5

$$\sin^2 p - \sin p + 1 = 1 - \sin^2 p$$
$$2\sin^2 p - \sin p = 0$$
$$\sin p (2\sin p - 1) = 0$$

Remember:
$$\sin^2 x + \cos^2 x = 1$$
so $\cos^2 x = 1 - \sin^2 x$

$\sin p = 0$ or $2\sin p - 1 = 0$

$p = 0, \pi, 2\pi$

We want $\frac{\pi}{2} < p < \pi$

$\sin p = \frac{1}{2}$

$$p = \pi - \frac{\pi}{6}$$
$$= \frac{5\pi}{6}.$$

We want $\frac{\pi}{2} < p < \pi$.

Exact value...

So $p = \frac{5\pi}{6}$.

SQP 1 Paper 2

1 See **Straight Lines** (a) §7, (b) §8, (c) §10, (d) §3

a $N = \text{midpoint}_{AB} = \left(\frac{2+10}{2}, \frac{1+1}{2}\right) = (6,1)$.

$m_{CN} = \frac{1-7}{6-4} = \frac{-6}{2} = -3$.

So the equation is $\quad y - 1 = -3(x-6) \quad$ using $N(6,1)$

$$y - 1 = -3x + 18$$

$$3x + y - 19 = 0.$$

b $m_{BC} = \frac{7-1}{4-10} = \frac{6}{-6} = -1$. So $m_{AD} = 1$ since $AD \perp BC$.

$$(\text{i.e. } m_{BC} \times m_{AD} = -1)$$

So the equation is $\quad y - 1 = 1(x-2) \quad$ using $A(2,1)$.

$$x - y - 1 = 0.$$

c Solve simultaneously...

Method 1 Eliminating y:

$$3x + y - 19 = 0 \quad \text{———} \quad ①$$
$$x - y - 1 = 0 \quad \text{———} \quad ②$$

$① + ②$: $4x - 20 = 0$

$$x = 5$$

Method 2 Rearrange both equations for y and equate:

$$19 - 3x = x - 1$$
$$4x = 20$$
$$x = 5$$

When $x = 5$, $y = 5 - 1 = 4$. So P has coordinates $(5,4)$.

d $m_{PQ} = \frac{1-4}{8-5} = \frac{-3}{3} = -1 = m_{BC}$ from part (b).

So PQ and BC are parallel.

2

See **Vectors** §7, §3 and §12

a The lengths of the edges are as follows...

- A and B only differ in the first coordinate, so the length of AB is the difference in the first coordinate.

- Similar for BC = AD.

- G has coordinates $(2,7,9)$ so GC = AE = 5.

> Note: It's not necessary to show any of this working.

So $AB = 1$, $AD = 4$, $AE = 5$.

b $\vec{HB} = \underline{b} - \underline{h} = \begin{pmatrix} 2 \\ 3 \\ 4 \end{pmatrix} - \begin{pmatrix} 1 \\ 7 \\ 9 \end{pmatrix} = \begin{pmatrix} 1 \\ -4 \\ -5 \end{pmatrix}$.

$\vec{HC} = \underline{c} - \underline{h} = \begin{pmatrix} 2 \\ 7 \\ 4 \end{pmatrix} - \begin{pmatrix} 1 \\ 7 \\ 9 \end{pmatrix} = \begin{pmatrix} 1 \\ 0 \\ -5 \end{pmatrix}$.

> Remember:
> $\vec{AB} = \underline{b} - \underline{a}$

> You could just write these down from the diagram.

$|\vec{HB}| = \sqrt{1^2 + (-4)^2 + (-5)^2} = \sqrt{42}$.

$|\vec{HC}| = \sqrt{1^2 + (-5)^2} = \sqrt{26}$.

Method 1 $\quad \cos B\hat{H}C = \dfrac{\vec{HB} \cdot \vec{HC}}{|\vec{HB}||\vec{HC}|}$

> Using:
> $\underline{a} \cdot \underline{b} = |\underline{a}||\underline{b}|\cos\theta$

$\qquad\qquad\quad = \dfrac{1 \times 1 - 4 \times 0 - 5 \times (-5)}{\sqrt{42}\sqrt{26}}$

$\qquad B\hat{H}C = \cos^{-1}\left(\dfrac{26}{\sqrt{42}\sqrt{26}}\right)$

$\qquad\qquad\quad = 38 \cdot 11° \text{ (to 2 d.p.)}$

$\qquad\qquad\quad \text{OR} \quad 0 \cdot 665 \text{ rads (to 3 d.p.)}$

cont...

Method 2   We have:

So $\cos B\hat{H}C = \dfrac{42 + 26 - 16}{2\sqrt{42}\sqrt{26}}$

(Remember the cosine rule:
$\cos A = \dfrac{b^2 + c^2 - a^2}{2bc}$)

$= \dfrac{26}{\sqrt{42}\sqrt{26}}$

So $B\hat{H}C = 38.11°$ (to 2 d.p.) or 0.665 rads (to 3 d.p.)

---

3   *See **Wave Functions** §2 and §5*

a $5\sin x° - 12\cos x° = k\sin(x° - a°)$

$= k\sin x° \cos a° - k\cos x° \sin a°.$

$= (k\cos a°)\sin x° - (k\sin a°)\cos x°.$

Comparing coefficients: $k\sin a° = 12$ $\begin{array}{c|c} S^{\checkmark} & A^{\checkmark\checkmark} \\ \hline T & C_{\checkmark} \end{array}$
$k\cos a° = 5$

So $k = \sqrt{12^2 + 5^2}$ and $\tan a° = \dfrac{k\sin a°}{k\cos a°} = \dfrac{12}{5}$
$= \sqrt{169}$
$= 13$ $a = \tan^{-1}\left(\dfrac{12}{5}\right) = 67.38$ (to 2 d.p.)

So $5\sin x° - 12\cos x° = 13\sin(x° - 67.38°)$.

b $5\sin x° - 12\cos x° = 6.5$
$13\sin(x° - 67.38°) = 6.5$
$\sin(x° - 67.38°) = 0.5$ $\begin{array}{c|c} S^{\checkmark} & A^{\checkmark} \\ \hline T & C \end{array}$ $\sin^{-1}(0.5) = 30°$

$x - 67.38 = 30$ or $180 - 30$

$x = 97.38$ or 217.38 (to 2 d.p.)

4

(a) See **Differentiation** §5
(b) See **Circles** §5
(c) See **Vectors** §10

a $\dfrac{dy}{dx} = 4x - 2$. $\left(\text{Remember: } \dfrac{dy}{dx} = m_{tangent}\right)$

When $x = 1$, $m_{tangent} = 4 \times 1 - 2 = 2$.

Using $P(1,3)$, the equation is $\quad y - 3 = 2(x - 1)$

$$y - 3 = 2x - 2$$

$$2x - y + 1 = 0.$$

b Put $y = 2x + 1$ into the equation of the circle...

$$x^2 + (2x + 1)^2 + 8(2x + 1) + 11 = 0$$

$$x^2 + 4x^2 + 4x + 1 + 16x + 8 + 11 = 0$$

$$5x^2 + 20x + 20 = 0$$

$$x^2 + 4x + 4 = 0$$

$$(x + 2)^2 = 0$$

$$x = -2.$$

$\left(\text{You could have used the discriminant to show that there is only one solution}\right)$

Since there is only one solution, there is only one point of intersection. Hence the line is a tangent to the circle.

When $x = -2$, $y = 2 \times (-2) + 1 = -4 + 1 = -3$.

So the point of contact is $Q(-2, -3)$.

cont...

c QP has equation $y = 2x + 1$.
So when $x = 0$, $y = 1$.

P(1,3)

T(0,1)

Q(-2,-3)

Method 1

$\overrightarrow{TP} = \begin{pmatrix} 1 \\ 2 \end{pmatrix}$, $\overrightarrow{QT} = \begin{pmatrix} 2 \\ 4 \end{pmatrix} = 2\overrightarrow{TP}$

So T divides $\overrightarrow{QP}$ in the ratio $2:1$.

Method 2

By Pythagoras's Theorem:

$x^2 = 2^2 + 1^2$, so $x = \sqrt{5}$.

$y^2 = 4^2 + 2^2$, so $y = \sqrt{20} = 2\sqrt{5}$.

So T divides $\overrightarrow{QP}$ in the ratio $2:1$.

5

*(a) See **Integration** §6*
*(b) See **Differentiation** §12 or **Polynomials and Quadratics** §3*

a Points of intersection...

$$x^2 = 6x + 16$$
$$x^2 - 6x - 16 = 0$$
$$(x + 2)(x - 8) = 0$$
$$x + 2 = 0 \quad \text{or} \quad x - 8 = 0.$$
$$x = -2 \qquad x = 8$$

cont...

The shaded area is given by

$$\int_{-2}^{8} (\text{upper} - \text{lower})\, dx$$

$$= \int_{-2}^{8} (6x + 16 - x^2)\, dx$$

$$= \left[3x^2 + 16x - \frac{x^3}{3} \right]_{-2}^{8}$$

$$= \left(3 \times 8^2 + 16 \times 8 - \frac{8^3}{3} \right) - \left(3 \times (-2)^2 + 16 \times (-2) - \frac{(-2)^3}{3} \right)$$

$$= \frac{448}{3} + \frac{52}{3}$$

$$= \frac{500}{3} \quad \left(= 166\tfrac{2}{3} \right).$$

So the area is $\frac{500}{3}$ square units.

b We want to maximise $A(x) = -5x^2 + 30x + 80$.

Method 1 Stationary points exist where $A'(x) = 0$.

$$A'(x) = -10x + 30 = 0$$
$$x = \frac{30}{10}$$
$$= 3$$

Then $A(3) = -5 \times 3^2 + 30 \times 3 + 80 = 125$.

Nature:

x	3^-	3	3^+
$A'(x)$	$+$	0	$-$
Sketch	$\diagup$	$-$	$\diagdown$

So the maximum area is 125 square units.

cont...

Method 2 Completing the square...

$$A(x) = -5(x^2 - 6x) + 80$$
$$= -5(x-3)^2 + 45 + 80$$
$$= -5(x-3)^2 + 125.$$

The turning point is $(3, 125)$ and is a maximum since $-5 < 0$ so the parabola is concave down $(\cap)$.

So the maximum area is 125 square units.

As a proportion of the total area it is $\dfrac{125}{500/3} = \dfrac{375}{500} = \dfrac{3}{4}$.

6

*See **Exponentials and Logarithms** §5*

a) $A(1600) = \frac{1}{2}A_0$ After 1600 years, the amount has halved.

$$A_0 e^{-1600k} = \frac{1}{2}A_0$$

$$e^{-1600k} = \frac{1}{2}$$

$$-1600k = \log_e\left(\frac{1}{2}\right)$$ Taking $\log_e$ on both sides

$$k = -\frac{\log_e\left(\frac{1}{2}\right)}{1600}$$

$$= 0.0004332 \ (\text{to 4 s.f.})$$

b) Method 1 $A(3200) = A_0 \times e^{(-0.0004332 \times 3200)}$ *(Remember the brackets on your calculator.)*

$$= 0.250 A_0. \ (\text{to 3 d.p.})$$

So after 3200 years, we are left with 25%.

Method 2   Let $A_0 = 100$ since we start with 100%.

Then $A(3200) = 100 e^{(-0.0004332 \times 3200)}$

$$= 25.001 \ (\text{to 3 d.p.})$$

$$= 25 \ (\text{to the nearest whole number})$$

So after 3200 years, we are left with 25%.

7

See **Trigonometry** §4

From the diagram, $\cos 2x° = \dfrac{adj.}{hyp.} = \dfrac{6}{10} = \dfrac{3}{5}$.

$$\cos 2x° = 2\cos^2 x° - 1 = \frac{3}{5}$$

$$2\cos^2 x° = \frac{8}{5}$$

$$\cos^2 x° = \frac{8}{10}$$

$$\cos^2 x = \frac{4}{5}$$

$$\cos x° = \pm \frac{2}{\sqrt{5}}.$$

Since x is acute, $\cos x° > 0$ so $\cos x° = \dfrac{2}{\sqrt{5}}$.

From the diagram, $\cos x° = \dfrac{6}{BD}$

$$BD = \frac{6}{2/\sqrt{5}}$$

$$= 3\sqrt{5} \quad units.$$

1

See **Sequences** §2

$u_{11} = 0.3\,u_{10} + 6 = 0.3 \times 10 + 6 = 3 + 6 = 9.$

$u_{12} = 0.3\,u_{11} + 6 = 0.3 \times 9 + 6 = 2.7 + 6 = 8.7.$

C

2

See **Circles** §1

Since the x-axis is a tangent, the radius is 6 units.

Therefore the equation is

$$(x - (-7))^2 + (y - 6)^2 = 6^2$$
$$(x + 7)^2 + (y - 6)^2 = 36.$$

The circle with centre (a, b) and radius r has equation:
$$(x-a)^2 + (y-b)^2 = r^2.$$

D

3

See **Vectors** §13

$\underline{u} \cdot \underline{v} = (k \times 0) + (-1 \times 4) + (1 \times k)$

$\qquad = k - 4.$

Since $\underline{u}$ and $\underline{v}$ are perpendicular, $\underline{u} \cdot \underline{v} = 0.$

So $k - 4 = 0$ i.e. $k = 4.$

C

4

See **Sequences** §4

Method 1 $\quad l = \dfrac{b}{1-a}$ with $a = 0.4$ and $b = -240.$

$l = \dfrac{-240}{1 - 0.4} = -\dfrac{240}{0.6} = -\dfrac{2400}{6} = -400.$

Method 2 $\quad$ As $n \to \infty$, $u_{n+1} = u_n = l.$

So $\quad l = 0.4l - 240$

$\qquad 0.6l = -240$

$\qquad l = -\dfrac{240}{0.6} = -\dfrac{2400}{6} = -400.$

B

5

See **Circles** §6

$m_{radius} = \dfrac{9-5}{7-2} = \dfrac{4}{5}$.

So $m_{tangent} = -\dfrac{5}{4}$ since the radius and tangent are perpendicular.

The equation of the tangent is:

$$y - 9 = -\frac{5}{4}(x - 7) \qquad \text{using point } (7,9)$$

A

6

See **Trigonometry** §1

$2\sin x - \sqrt{3} = 0$

$\sin x = \dfrac{\sqrt{3}}{2}$

$\begin{array}{c|c} \pi - a & a \\ \hline \sqrt{S} & A \\ \hline T & C \\ \hline \pi + a & 2\pi - a \end{array}$ Not here since $\frac{\pi}{2} \leqslant x \leqslant \pi$.

$x = \pi - \dfrac{\pi}{3}$

$= \dfrac{2\pi}{3}$

$a = \sin^{-1}\left(\dfrac{\sqrt{3}}{2}\right)$

$= \dfrac{\pi}{3}$.

Exact value ...

B

7

See **Straight Lines** §3

$m = \tan 135°$
$= -\tan 45°$
$= -1$.

Exact value ...

C

8

See **Functions and Graphs** §10

$y = -f(x-2)$ is $y = f(x)$ reflected in the x-axis and then shifted 2 places to the right.

D

9

See **Trigonometry** §3

$\sin a = \dfrac{\text{opp.}}{\text{hyp.}} = \dfrac{3}{5}$. So we have:

Using Pythagoras's Theorem.

So $\cos a = \dfrac{\text{adj.}}{\text{hyp.}} = \dfrac{4}{5}$.

Now $\sin(x+a) = \sin x \cos a + \cos x \sin a$
$= \dfrac{4}{5}\sin x + \dfrac{3}{5}\cos x$.

B

2008

10

See **Polynomials and Quadratics** §2

The discriminant is $b^2 - 4ac = 1 - 4 \times 1 \times 1 = -3$.
Since $b^2 - 4ac < 0$, the roots are <u>not</u> real and <u>not</u> equal.

A

11

See **Vectors** §10

$\overrightarrow{EP} = \underline{p} - \underline{e} = \begin{pmatrix} 1 \\ 5 \\ 7 \end{pmatrix} - \begin{pmatrix} -2 \\ -1 \\ 4 \end{pmatrix} = \begin{pmatrix} 3 \\ 6 \\ 3 \end{pmatrix}$

$\overrightarrow{PF} = \underline{f} - \underline{p} = \begin{pmatrix} 7 \\ 17 \\ 13 \end{pmatrix} - \begin{pmatrix} 1 \\ 5 \\ 7 \end{pmatrix} = \begin{pmatrix} 6 \\ 12 \\ 6 \end{pmatrix} = 2\overrightarrow{EP}$

So $\dfrac{EP}{PF} = \dfrac{1}{2}$, i.e. P divides EF in the ratio $1:2$.

B

12

See **Vectors** §5

From the diagram, $\overrightarrow{VT} = \overrightarrow{VW} + \overrightarrow{WS} + \overrightarrow{ST}$
$$= -\underline{f} - \underline{h} + \underline{g}$$
$$= -\underline{f} + \underline{g} - \underline{h}.$$

C

13

See **Polynomials and Quadratics** §5

Since the parabola crosses the x-axis at 1 and 4, the equation has the form
$$y = k(x-1)(x-4).$$
Since $(0,12)$ lies on the parabola,
$$12 = k \times (-1) \times (-4)$$
$$k = \frac{12}{4}$$
$$= 3.$$
So the equation is $y = 3(x-1)(x-4)$.

A

14

See **Further Calculus** §6

$$\int 4\sin(2x+3)\,dx = -4 \times \tfrac{1}{2}\cos(2x+3) + c$$
$$= -2\cos(2x+3) + c.$$

Using:
$$\int \sin(ax+b)\,dx$$
$$= -\tfrac{1}{a}\cos(ax+b) + c$$

B

15

See **Further Calculus** §4

Using the chain rule,

$$\frac{d}{dx}\left(x^3+4\right)^2 = 2\left(x^3+4\right) \times \frac{d}{dx}\left(x^3+4\right)$$

$$= 2\left(x^3+4\right) \times \left(3x^2\right)$$

$$= 6x^2\left(x^3+4\right).$$

C

16

See **Polynomials and Quadratics** §3

2008

Method 1   Compensating...

$$2x^2+4x+7 = 2\left(x^2+2x\right)+7$$

$$= 2\left(x+1\right)^2-2+7 = 2\left(x+1\right)^2+5. \quad \text{So } q = 5.$$

This gives the correct x^2 and x terms, and an extra 2.

Take off this extra 2.

Method 2   Comparing coefficients...

$$2x^2+4x+7 = 2\left(x+p\right)^2+q$$

$$= 2x^2+4px+2p^2+q$$

So $4p = 4$ and $2p^2+q = 7$

$\quad\quad\quad p = 1$ $\quad\quad\quad\quad\quad\quad q = 7-2p^2$

$\quad\quad\quad\quad\quad\quad\quad\quad\quad\quad\quad = 5$

A

17

See **Functions and Graphs** §2

We need $9-x^2 \geqslant 0$

$\quad\quad\quad\quad x^2 \leqslant 9$

$\quad\quad -3 \leqslant x \leqslant 3.$

Remember: we can't take the square root of a negative number.

C

18

See **Vectors** §14

$$\underline{q} \cdot (\underline{p} + \underline{q}) = \underline{q} \cdot \underline{p} + \underline{q} \cdot \underline{q}$$
$$= \underline{p} \cdot \underline{q} + |\underline{q}|^2$$
$$= 10 + 4^2$$
$$= 26.$$

Remember:
- $\underline{a} \cdot \underline{b} = \underline{b} \cdot \underline{a}$
- $\underline{a} \cdot \underline{a} = |\underline{a}|^2$

C

19

See **Functions and Graphs** §5

Since $(3, 54)$ lies on the curve,
$$54 = 2m^3$$
$$m^3 = 27$$
$$m = \sqrt[3]{27}$$
$$= 3$$

B

20

See **Functions and Graphs** §6

Since $(q, 2)$ lies on the curve,
$$2 = \log_3(q - 4)$$
$$q - 4 = 3^2$$
$$q = 9 + 4$$
$$= 13.$$

Remember:
$$y = \log_a x$$
$$\Leftrightarrow x = a^y$$

D

21

(a) See **Differentiation** §7 and §8
(b) See **Polynomials and Quadratics** §9
(c) See **Differentiation** §9

a Stationary points exist where $f'(x) = 0$

$$f'(x) = 3x^2 - 3 = 0$$
$$3x^2 = 3$$
$$x = \pm 1.$$

When $x = -1$, $y = (-1)^3 - 3 \times (-1) + 2$
$$= -1 + 3 + 2$$
$$= 4 \qquad (-1, 4)$$

When $x = 1$, $y = 1 - 3 + 2 = 0 \qquad (1, 0).$

cont...

Method 1 Nature table:

x	-1^-	-1	-1^+	1^-	1	1^+
$f'(x)$	$+$	0	$-$	$-$	0	$+$
Sketch	$\diagup$	$-$	$\diagdown$	$\diagdown$	$-$	$\diagup$

Method 2 Second derivative test: $f''(x) = 6x$

$$f''(-1) = -6 < 0 \quad \text{and} \quad f''(1) = 6 > 0.$$

So $(-1, 4)$ is a maximum turning point
$(1, 0)$ is a minimum turning point.

b **i** **Method 1** From part (a), $f(1) = 0$ (ie $x = 1$ is a root) and so $(x-1)$ is a factor.

Method 2 Using synthetic division...

$$
\begin{array}{r|rrr}
1 & 1 & 0 & -3 & 2 \\
  &   & 1 & 1 & -2 \\
\hline
  & 1 & 1 & -2 & \boxed{0}
\end{array}
$$

Since the remainder is 0, $x = 1$ is a root so $(x-1)$ is a factor.

ii $x^3 - 3x + 2 = (x-1)(x^2 + x - 2) \longleftarrow$ Either by inspection or from the bottom row of the table.
$\qquad\qquad\quad = (x-1)(x-1)(x+2)$

c x-axis (i.e. $y = 0$). From above, $x = -2, 1$.
$\qquad$ Hence the curve crosses the x-axis at $(-2, 0)$ and $(1, 0)$.

y-axis (i.e. $x = 0$). $f(0) = 2$
$\qquad$ Hence the curve crosses the y-axis at $(0, 2)$.

Using this information, and the stationary points,

2008

22

*(a) See **Differentiation** §5, (b) See **Straight Lines** §6*

a

$$\frac{dy}{dx} = 3x^2 - 12x + 8$$

Remember: $\frac{dy}{dx} = m_{tangent}$

So $3x^2 - 12x + 8 = -1$

$3x^2 - 12x + 9 = 0$

$x^2 - 4x + 3 = 0$

$(x-1)(x-3) = 0$

$x = 1$ or $x = 3$

When $x = 1$, $y = 1 - 6 + 8 = 3$

When $x = 3$, $y = 3^3 - 6 \times 3^2 + 8 \times 3 = 27 - 54 + 24 = -3$.

So the points are $(1,3)$ and $(3,-3)$.

b The line $y = 4 - x$ has gradient -1.

So A must be one of the points found in part (a).

Remember: the line $y = mx + c$ has gradient m.

The equation is only satisfied by $(1,3)$, since $3 = 4 - 1$, and so A is the point $(1,3)$.

23

*(a) See **Functions and Graphs** §3*
*(b) See **Exponentials and Logarithms** §5*

a $h(f(x)) = h(x^2 - x + 10) = \log_2(x^2 - x + 10)$.

$h(g(x)) = h(5 - x) = \log_2(5 - x)$.

b $\log_2(x^2 - x + 10) - \log_2(5 - x) = 3$

$$\log_2\left(\frac{x^2 - x + 10}{5 - x}\right) = 3$$

$$\frac{x^2 - x + 10}{5 - x} = 2^3$$

$x^2 - x + 10 = 40 - 8x$

$x^2 + 7x - 30 = 0$

$(x + 10)(x - 3) = 0$

$x = -10$ or $x = 3$.

Remember:
- $\log_a x - \log_a y = \log_a \frac{x}{y}$
- $\log_a x = y \Leftrightarrow x = a^y$

1

See **Straight Lines** – (a) §9, (b) §7, (c) §10

a)

$$\text{midpoint}_{BC} = \left(\frac{-3+5}{2}, \frac{-1-5}{2}\right) = (1, -3).$$

$$m_{BC} = \frac{-5-(-1)}{5-(-3)} = -\frac{4}{8} = -\frac{1}{2}. \quad \text{So } m_{\perp} = 2 \text{ since } m_{BC} \times m_{\perp} = -1.$$

So the equation is
$$y + 3 = 2(x - 1) \quad \text{using point } (1, -3)$$
$$y + 3 = 2x - 2$$
$$y = 2x - 5$$

b)

$$\text{midpoint}_{AB} = \left(\frac{7-3}{2}, \frac{9-1}{2}\right) = (2, 4).$$

$$m_{med} = \frac{-5-4}{5-2} = -\frac{9}{3} = -3.$$

So the equation is
$$y + 5 = -3(x - 5) \quad \text{using } C(5, -5).$$
$$y + 5 = -3x + 15$$
$$y = -3x + 10.$$

c) Solve simultaneously...

Method 1 Eliminating y:
$$y = 2x - 5 \quad \text{———} \quad ①$$
$$y = -3x + 10. \quad \text{———} \quad ②$$
$$① - ②: \quad 5x - 15 = 0$$
$$x = 3.$$

Method 2 Equating:
$$2x - 5 = -3x + 10$$
$$5x = 15$$
$$x = 3.$$

When $x = 3$, $y = 2 \times 3 - 5 = 1$. So the point of intersection is $(3, 1)$

2

See **Vectors** – (a) §7 and §10, (b) §7, (c) §12

2008

a From the diagram, $A(8,0,0)$, $C(0,4,0)$, $E(8,0,6)$ and $G(0,4,6)$.

So $p = \underline{a} + \frac{2}{3}\overrightarrow{AE} = \begin{pmatrix} 8 \\ 0 \\ 0 \end{pmatrix} + \frac{2}{3}\begin{pmatrix} 0 \\ 0 \\ 6 \end{pmatrix} = \begin{pmatrix} 8 \\ 0 \\ 4 \end{pmatrix}$

$q = \underline{c} + \frac{1}{2}\overrightarrow{CG} = \begin{pmatrix} 0 \\ 4 \\ 0 \end{pmatrix} + \frac{1}{2}\begin{pmatrix} 0 \\ 0 \\ 6 \end{pmatrix} = \begin{pmatrix} 0 \\ 4 \\ 3 \end{pmatrix}$.

> Note: you don't need to show this working.

Hence $P(8,0,4)$ and $Q(0,4,3)$.

b $\overrightarrow{PQ} = q - p = \begin{pmatrix} 0 \\ 4 \\ 3 \end{pmatrix} - \begin{pmatrix} 8 \\ 0 \\ 4 \end{pmatrix} = \begin{pmatrix} -8 \\ 4 \\ -1 \end{pmatrix}$

$\overrightarrow{PA} = \underline{a} - p = \begin{pmatrix} 8 \\ 0 \\ 0 \end{pmatrix} - \begin{pmatrix} 8 \\ 0 \\ 4 \end{pmatrix} = \begin{pmatrix} 0 \\ 0 \\ -4 \end{pmatrix}$

> Remember:
> $\overrightarrow{AB} = \underline{b} - \underline{a}$.

c $|\overrightarrow{PQ}| = \sqrt{(-8)^2 + 4^2 + (-1)^2} = \sqrt{81} = 9$.

$|\overrightarrow{PA}| = \sqrt{(-4)^2} = 4$

Method 1 $\cos Q\hat{P}A = \dfrac{\overrightarrow{PQ}.\overrightarrow{PA}}{|\overrightarrow{PQ}||\overrightarrow{PA}|}$

> Using:
> $\underline{a}.\underline{b} = |\underline{a}||\underline{b}|\cos\theta$

$= \dfrac{-8\times 0 + 4\times 0 - 1\times(-4)}{9 \times 4}$

$= \dfrac{1}{9}$

$Q\hat{P}A = \cos^{-1}\left(\dfrac{1}{9}\right)$

$= 83.62°$ (to 2 d.p.)

or 1.459 rads (to 3 d.p.)

Method 2 $|\overrightarrow{AQ}| = \left|\begin{pmatrix} -8 \\ 4 \\ 3 \end{pmatrix}\right| = \sqrt{89}$.

$\cos Q\hat{P}A = \dfrac{81 + 16 - 89}{2\times 9\times 4}$

$= \dfrac{1}{9}$

> Remember the cosine rule:
> $\cos A = \dfrac{b^2 + c^2 - a^2}{2bc}$

So $Q\hat{P}A = 83.62°$ (to 2 d.p.) or 1.459 rads (to 3 d.p.)

3

(a) See **Functions and Graphs** §9 and §10
(b) See **Wave Functions** §2
(c) See **Further Calculus** §1

a i The amplitude is $\sqrt{7}$ so $p = \sqrt{7}$.

ii The amplitude is 3 but the sine graph has also been reflected in the x-axis.

Hence $q = -3$.

b $\begin{aligned} f(x) + g(x) &= \sqrt{7}\cos x - 3\sin x \\ &= k\cos(x + a) \\ &= k\cos x \cos a - k\sin x \sin a \\ &= (k\cos a)\cos x - (k\sin a)\sin x \end{aligned}$

Comparing coefficients: $\begin{aligned} k\sin a &= 3 \\ k\cos a &= \sqrt{7} \end{aligned}$

$\overset{\checkmark}{S}$	$A \overset{\checkmark\checkmark}{}$
T	$C\,\checkmark$

So $k = \sqrt{3^2 + \sqrt{7}^2}$ and $\tan a = \dfrac{k\sin a}{k\cos a} = \dfrac{3}{\sqrt{7}}$
$\quad = \sqrt{16}$
$\quad = 4$ $\qquad\qquad a = \tan^{-1}\left(\dfrac{3}{\sqrt{7}}\right) = 0.848$ (to 3 d.p.)

So $f(x) + g(x) = 4\cos(x + 0.848)$.

c $\begin{aligned} f'(x) + g'(x) &= \frac{d}{dx}\big(f(x) + g(x)\big) \\ &= \frac{d}{dx}\big(4\cos(x + 0.848)\big) \qquad \left(\text{Using: } \frac{d}{dx}\cos x = -\sin x.\right) \\ &= -4\sin(x + 0.848). \end{aligned}$

4

See **Circles** – (a) §3, (b) §1 and §7, (c) §4

a Comparing with $x^2 + y^2 + 2gx + 2fy + c = 0$,
$\quad 2g = 8, \quad 2f = 4 \quad$ and $\quad c = -38$
$\quad\ g = 4 \qquad f = 2$.

The centre is $(-4, -2)$.

The circle $x^2 + y^2 + 2gx + 2fy + c = 0$ has centre $(-g, -f)$ and radius $\sqrt{g^2 + f^2 - c}$.

The radius is $\sqrt{16 + 4 + 38} = \sqrt{58}$ units.

cont...

b The circle $(x-4)^2 + (y-6)^2 = 26$ has centre $(4,6)$ and radius $\sqrt{26}$ units.

The distance between the centres is
$$d = \sqrt{(4+4)^2 + (6+2)^2} = \sqrt{128} = 8\sqrt{2} \text{ units.}$$

The sum of the two radii is larger than d since:
$$\sqrt{58} + \sqrt{26} = \underbrace{\sqrt{13}\sqrt{2}}_{>3} + \underbrace{\sqrt{29}\sqrt{2}}_{>5} > 8\sqrt{2} = d.$$

Since the distance between the centres is less than the sum of the radii, the circles intersect.

c Put $y = 4 - x$ in the equation of one of the circles:
$$x^2 + (4-x)^2 + 8x + 4(4-x) - 38 = 0$$
$$x^2 + 16 - 8x + x^2 + 8x + 16 - 4x - 38 = 0$$
$$2x^2 - 4x - 6 = 0$$
$$x^2 - 2x - 3 = 0$$
$$(x+1)(x-3) = 0$$
$$x = -1 \text{ or } x = 3.$$

When $x = -1$, $y = 4 - (-1) = 5$.
When $x = 3$, $y = 4 - 3 = 1$.

So the points of intersection are $(-1,5)$ and $(3,1)$.

5

See **Trigonometry** §4 and §5

$$\cos 2x° + 2\sin x° = \sin^2 x°$$
$$1 - 2\sin^2 x° + 2\sin x° = \sin^2 x°$$
$$3\sin^2 x° - 2\sin x° - 1 = 0$$
$$(3\sin x° + 1)(\sin x° - 1) = 0$$

Using:
$$\cos 2A = 1 - 2\sin^2 A$$

$$3\sin x° + 1 = 0$$
$$\sin x° = -\frac{1}{3}$$

$$180-a \ | \ a$$
$$S \ | \ A$$
$$\sqrt{T} \ | \ C \checkmark$$
$$180+a \ | \ 360-a$$

or

$$\sin x° - 1 = 0$$
$$\sin x° = 1$$
$$x = 90$$

$$a = \sin^{-1}\left(\frac{1}{3}\right)$$
$$= 19.47 \text{ (to 2 d.p.)}$$

$$x = 180 + 19.47 \text{ or } 360 - 19.47 \text{ or } 90$$
$$= 199.47 \text{ or } 340.53 \text{ or } 90$$

6

(a) See **Straight Lines** §6
(b) See **Polynomials and Quadratics** §4 or **Differentiation** §12

a The line has gradient -2 and y-axis intercept 6.

So its equation is $y = -2x + 6$.

The length QR is the y-coordinate of the point on this line with x-coordinate t, i.e.

$$QR = -2t + 6 = 6 - 2t.$$

b The area of the rectangle is given by $A = \text{length} \times \text{breadth}$
$$= t(6 - 2t).$$

Method 1 Sketch $A = t(6 - 2t)$.

Crosses t-axis when $t(6 - 2t) = 0$

$$t = 0 \text{ or } 6 - 2t = 0$$
$$t = 3$$

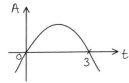

The parabola is concave down ($\cap$-shaped) because the coefficient of t^2 is negative.

The maximum lies mid-way between the roots, ie when $t = \frac{3}{2}$.

Method 2 $A = 6t - 2t^2$.

Stationary points exist where $\frac{dA}{dt} = 0$.

$$\frac{dA}{dt} = 6 - 4t = 0$$
$$4t = 6$$
$$t = \frac{3}{2}$$

Nature:

t	$\frac{3}{2}^-$	$\frac{3}{2}$	$\frac{3}{2}^+$
$\frac{dA}{dt}$	$+$	0	$-$
Sketch	$\diagup$	$-$	$\diagdown$

OR $\dfrac{d^2 A}{dt^2} = -4$

Hence $t = \frac{3}{2}$ gives the maximum area.

When $t = \frac{3}{2}$, $QR = 6 - 2 \times \frac{3}{2} = 3$.

Hence Q is $\left(\frac{3}{2}, 3\right)$.

2008

7

See **Integration** §7 or §6

First notice that the shaded area is symmetrical about the y-axis. So first calculate the area for $x > 0$, then double.

Method 1 Rearrange for x and integrate with respect to y.

$$y = 32 - 2x^2$$
$$2x^2 = 32 - y$$
$$x = \left(16 - \frac{y}{2}\right)^{1/2} \quad \text{(Only consider } x > 0.\text{)}$$

So half the shaded area is given by

$$\int_{14}^{24} \left(16 - \frac{1}{2}y\right)^{1/2} dy = \left[\frac{\left(16 - \frac{y}{2}\right)^{3/2}}{\frac{3}{2} \times \left(-\frac{1}{2}\right)}\right]_{14}^{24}$$

Remember:
$$\int (ax+b)^n dx = \frac{(ax+b)^{n+1}}{a(n+1)} + c$$

$$= \left[-\frac{4}{3}\sqrt{16 - \frac{y}{2}}^{\,3}\right]_{14}^{24}$$

$$= -\frac{4}{3}\sqrt{4}^{\,3} + \frac{4}{3}\sqrt{9}^{\,3}$$

$$= \frac{76}{3} \quad \left(= 25\frac{1}{3}\right)$$

Hence the shaded area is $\frac{152}{3}$ $\left(\text{or } 50\frac{2}{3}\right)$ square units.

cont...

Method 2

Find a and b.

a: $32 - 2x^2 = 24$

$2x^2 = 8$

$x = 2$

(Only consider $x > 0$.)

i.e. $a = 2$.

b: $32 - 2x^2 = 14$

$2x^2 = 18$

$x = 3$.

i.e. $b = 3$.

The shaded area between a and b is given by

$$\int_2^3 (\text{upper} - \text{lower})\, dx$$

$$= \int_2^3 (32 - 2x^2 - 14)\, dx$$

$$= \left[18x - \frac{2}{3} x^3 \right]_2^3$$

$$= 54 - \frac{2}{3} \times 27 - 36 + \frac{2}{3} \times 8$$

$$= \frac{16}{3} \quad \left(= 5\frac{1}{3} \right)$$

So the total shaded area is

$$2 \left(10 \times 2 + \frac{16}{3} \right) = \frac{152}{3} \quad \text{or} \quad 50\frac{2}{3} \text{ square units.}$$

2008

1
See **Straight Lines** §3

$$m_{PQ} = \frac{p - (-5)}{7 - 4} = \frac{p + 5}{3}.$$

So $\quad \frac{p+5}{3} = 3$

$\qquad p + 5 = 9$

$\qquad\quad p = 4.$

B

2
See **Sequences** §2

$u_1 = u_0 + 5 \ = -3 + 5 = 2$
$u_2 = u_1 + 5 \ = \ 2 + 5 \ = 7$

C

3
See **Straight Lines** §6 and §5

$3y = -2x + 1$
$y = -\frac{2}{3}x + \frac{1}{3}.$

So the gradient is $m = -\frac{2}{3}.$

Remember:
To extract the gradient,
rearrange to the form
$y = mx + c.$

Any line perpendicular has gradient $m_\perp = \frac{3}{2}$, since $m \times m_\perp = -1.$

C

4
See **Polynomials and Quadratics** §9

The remainder is
$$f(-3) = (-3)^2 - (-3)^2 - 5 \times (-3) - 3$$
$$= -27 - 9 + 15 - 3$$
$$= -24.$$

You could have used
synthetic division

A

SQP 2

5

See *Polynomials and Quadratics* §3

Method 1 Compensating...

$$x^2 - 16x + 27 = (x-8)^2 - 64 + 27 = (x-8)^2 - 37. \text{ So } q = -37.$$

> This gives the correct x^2 and x terms, and an extra 64

> Take off this extra 64

Method 2 Comparing coefficients...

$$x^2 - 16x + 27 = (x+p)^2 + q$$
$$= x^2 + 2px + p^2 + q.$$

So $\quad 2p = -16 \quad$ and $\quad p^2 + q = 27$
$$p = -8 \qquad\qquad q = 27 - p^2$$
$$= -37.$$

A

6

See *Further Calculus* §4

Using the chain rule,
$$\frac{d}{dx}(8-2x^2)^{2/3} = \frac{2}{3}(8-2x^2)^{-1/3} \times \frac{d}{dx}(8-2x^2)$$
$$= \frac{2}{3}(8-2x^2)^{-1/3}.(-4x)$$
$$= -\frac{8}{3}(8-2x^2)^{-1/3}.$$

A

7

See *Polynomials and Quadratics* §9

Since the remainder is zero, $(x-1)$ is a factor, i.e.
$$f(x) = (x-1)(x^2 - 4x - 5)$$
$$= (x-1)(x+1)(x-5).$$

D

8

See **Sequences** §4

Method 1 $l = \dfrac{b}{1-a}$ with $a = 0.4$ and $b = 3$

$l = \dfrac{3}{1-0.4} = \dfrac{3}{0.6} = \dfrac{30}{6} = 5.$

Method 2 As $n \to \infty$, $u_{n+1} = u_n = l$.

So $l = 0.4l + 3$

$0.6l = 3$

$l = \dfrac{3}{0.6} = \dfrac{30}{6} = 5.$

C

9

See **Trigonometry** §1

$\tan x = -\sqrt{3}$

$a = \tan^{-1}(\sqrt{3})$

$= \dfrac{\pi}{3}$

So $x = \pi - \dfrac{\pi}{3}$ or $2\pi - \dfrac{\pi}{3}$.

$= \dfrac{2\pi}{3}$ or $\dfrac{5\pi}{3}$.

Exact value...

C

10

See **Vectors** §10

$\overrightarrow{PQ} = q - p = \begin{pmatrix} -1 \\ 8 \\ 3 \end{pmatrix} - \begin{pmatrix} -3 \\ 4 \\ 7 \end{pmatrix} = \begin{pmatrix} 2 \\ 4 \\ -4 \end{pmatrix}$

$\overrightarrow{QR} = r - q = \begin{pmatrix} 0 \\ 10 \\ 1 \end{pmatrix} - \begin{pmatrix} -1 \\ 8 \\ 3 \end{pmatrix} = \begin{pmatrix} 1 \\ 2 \\ -2 \end{pmatrix}$

So $\overrightarrow{PQ} = 2\overrightarrow{QR}$, i.e. $\dfrac{PQ}{QR} = \dfrac{2}{1}$. Hence Q divides PR in the ratio $2:1$.

A

SQP 2

11

See **Straight Lines** §6 and §3

$2y = x$

$y = \frac{1}{2}x$. So $m = \frac{1}{2}$.

Since $m = \tan p°$,

$\tan p° = \frac{1}{2}$

$p = \tan^{-1}\left(\frac{1}{2}\right)$

Remember:
To extract the gradient, rearrange to the form $y = mx + c$.

A

12

See **Differentiation** §6

$g'(x) = x^2 + 2x + 1$

$= (x+1)^2$

$\geq 0.$

Since $g'(x) \geq 0$ for all x, g is never decreasing.

D

13

See **Exponentials and Logarithms** §3

$\log_2(x+1) - 2\log_2 3 = \log_2(x+1) - \log_2 3^2$

$= \log_2(x+1) - \log_2 9$

$= \log_2\left(\frac{x+1}{9}\right)$

Remember:
• $k\log_a x = \log_a x^k$.
• $\log_a x - \log_a y = \log_a \frac{x}{y}$.

A

14

See **Functions and Graphs** §10

$y = -g(x)$ is $y = g(x)$ reflected in the x-axis.

$3 - g(x) = -g(x) + 3$.

So $y = 3 - g(x)$ is $y = -g(x)$ shifted up by 3.

D

15

See **Vectors** §7 and §10

Method 1

$$t = p + \tfrac{1}{2}\overrightarrow{PQ}$$

$$= p + \tfrac{1}{2}(q - p)$$

$$= \tfrac{1}{2}(p + q)$$

$$= \tfrac{1}{2}\left(\begin{pmatrix} 1 \\ 3 \\ -1 \end{pmatrix} + \begin{pmatrix} 2 \\ 5 \\ 1 \end{pmatrix}\right)$$

$$= \begin{pmatrix} 3/2 \\ 4 \\ 0 \end{pmatrix}.$$

Method 2 Using the midpoint formula, T is

$$\left(\frac{1+2}{2}, \frac{3+5}{2}, \frac{-1+1}{2}\right) = \left(\frac{3}{2}, 4, 0\right).$$

So $t = \begin{pmatrix} 3/2 \\ 4 \\ 0 \end{pmatrix}.$

B

SQP 2

16

See **Vectors** §7

$$\overrightarrow{AD} = 4\overrightarrow{AB}$$

$$d - a = 4(b - a)$$

$$d = 4b - 4a + a$$

$$= 4b - 3a$$

$$= 4\begin{pmatrix} -1 \\ 8 \\ 3 \end{pmatrix} - 3\begin{pmatrix} -3 \\ 4 \\ 7 \end{pmatrix}$$

$$= \begin{pmatrix} -4 \\ 32 \\ 12 \end{pmatrix} - \begin{pmatrix} -9 \\ 12 \\ 21 \end{pmatrix}$$

$$= \begin{pmatrix} 5 \\ 20 \\ -9 \end{pmatrix}.$$ So D has coordinates $(5, 20, -9)$. **D**

17

See **Polynomials and Quadratics** §5

Since $(3, -18)$ lies on the parabola,

$$-18 = k \times 3 \times (3-6)$$
$$-18 = -9k$$
$$k = 2.$$

C

18

See **Further Calculus** §4

$$\frac{dy}{dx} = 3 \times (-5)\sin 5x$$
$$= -15\sin 5x.$$

Using: $\frac{d}{dx}(\cos ax) = -a\sin ax.$

B

SQP 2

19

See **Further Calculus** §5

$$\int (4x+1)^{1/2}\, dx = \frac{(4x+1)^{3/2}}{4 \times \frac{3}{2}} + c$$
$$= \frac{1}{6}(4x+1)^{3/2} + c.$$

Remember:
$$\int (ax+b)^n\, dx = \frac{(ax+b)^{n+1}}{a(n+1)} + c$$

A

20

See **Integration** §4

$$\int_0^1 (3x+1)^{-1/2}\, dx = \left[\frac{2}{3}\sqrt{3x+1}\right]_0^1$$
$$= \frac{2}{3} \times 2 - \frac{2}{3} \times 1$$
$$= \frac{2}{3}.$$

A

21

See **Differentiation** – (a) §7 and §8, (b) §9

a Stationary points exist where $\frac{dy}{dx} = 0$.

$$\frac{dy}{dx} = 3x^2 + 6x - 9 = 0$$
$$x^2 + 2x - 3 = 0$$
$$(x+3)(x-1) = 0$$
$$x = -3 \quad \text{or} \quad x = 1$$

When $x = -3$, $\quad y = (-3)^3 + 3 \times (-3)^2 - 9 \times (-3) + 5$
$$= -27 + 27 + 27 + 5$$
$$= 32. \qquad (-3, 32)$$

When $x = 1$, $\quad y = 1 + 3 - 9 + 5 = 0 \qquad (1, 0)$

Method 1 Nature table:

x	-3^-	-3	-3^+	1^-	1	1^+
$(x+3)$	$-$	0	$+$	$+$		$+$
$(x-1)$	$-$		$-$	$-$	0	$+$
$\frac{dy}{dx}$	$+$	0	$-$	$-$	0	$+$
Sketch	/	—	\	\	_	/

Method 2 Second derivative test: $\frac{d^2y}{dx^2} = 6x + 6$.

$$f''(-3) = -12 < 0 \quad \text{and} \quad f''(1) = 12 > 0$$

So $(-3, 32)$ is a maximum turning point
$(1, 0)$ is a minimum turning point.

b When $x = 0$, $y = 5$. So $(0, 5)$ lies on the curve.
Using the given information, and the stationary points,

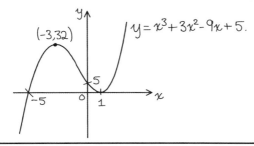

$y = x^3 + 3x^2 - 9x + 5$.

SQP 2

22

See **Exponentials and Logarithms** §5

$\log_x 8 + \log_x 4 = 5$
$\log_x 32 = 5$
$x^5 = 32$
$x = \sqrt[5]{32}$
$= 2.$

Remember:
• $\log_a u + \log_a v = \log_a uv$
• $\log_a u = v \Leftrightarrow a^v = u$

23

See **Trigonometry** §4 and §5

$\sin 2x - \cos x = 0$
$2\sin x \cos x - \cos x = 0$
$\cos x (2\sin x - 1) = 0$

$\cos x = 0$　or　$2\sin x - 1 = 0$
$\sin x = \dfrac{1}{2}$

$x = \dfrac{\pi}{2}$　or　$\dfrac{3\pi}{2}$　or　$\dfrac{\pi}{6}$　or　$\dfrac{5\pi}{6}$.

Using: $\sin 2A = 2\sin A \cos A$

$\begin{array}{c|c} \pi - a & a \\ \sqrt{S} & A\sqrt{} \\ \hline T & C \\ \pi + a & 2\pi - a \end{array}$

$a = \sin^{-1}\left(\dfrac{1}{2}\right)$
$= \dfrac{\pi}{6}$

Exact value...

24

See **Trigonometry** §3 and §4

From the diagram: $\hat{DEA} = 2x + 90$.

So $\cos(\hat{DEA}^\circ) = \cos(2x^\circ + 90^\circ)$
$= -\sin(2x^\circ)$
$= -2\sin x^\circ \cos x^\circ$
$= -2 \times \dfrac{1}{\sqrt{10}} \times \dfrac{3}{\sqrt{10}}$
$= -\dfrac{6}{10} = -\dfrac{3}{5}.$

Remember: $\cos(u + 90^\circ)$
$= -\sin u^\circ.$

Note: you could have used the addition formula.

By Pythagoras's Theorem:
$l^2 = 3^2 + 1^2$
$l = \sqrt{10}.$

25

See *Integration* §3

$$f(x) = \int f'(x)\,dx$$
$$= \int 6x\,(x-2)\,dx$$
$$= \int \left(6x^2 - 12x\right)\,dx$$
$$= \frac{6x^3}{3} - \frac{12x^2}{2} + c$$
$$= 2x^3 - 6x^2 + c.$$

We know $f(1) = 4$, i.e. $2 \times 1^3 - 6 \times 1^2 + c = 4$
$$-4 + c = 4$$
$$c = 8.$$

So $f(x) = 2x^3 - 6x^2 + 8$.

SQP 2

SQP 2 Paper 2

1

See **Vectors** §12

$$|\vec{QP}| = \sqrt{(-1)^2 + 3^2 + (-2)^2} = \sqrt{1+9+4} = \sqrt{14}$$

$$|\vec{QR}| = \sqrt{(-5)^2 + 1^2 + 1^2} = \sqrt{25+1+1} = \sqrt{27}$$

$$\vec{QP}.\vec{QR} = -1 \times (-5) + 3 \times 1 - 2 \times 1 = 5 + 3 - 2 = 6.$$

$$\cos P\hat{Q}R = \frac{\vec{QP}.\vec{QR}}{|\vec{QP}||\vec{QR}|}$$

Using:
$$\underline{a}.\underline{b} = |\underline{a}||\underline{b}|\cos\theta$$

$$= \frac{6}{\sqrt{14}\sqrt{27}}$$

$$P\hat{Q}R = \cos^{-1}\left(\frac{6}{\sqrt{14}\sqrt{27}}\right)$$

$$= 72.02° \quad \text{(to 2 d.p.)}$$

$$\underline{\text{or} \quad 1.257 \text{ rads}} \quad \text{(to 3 d.p.)}$$

2

See **Polynomials and Quadratics** §2

Given $2x^2 + px - 3 = 0$, let $a = 2$, $b = p$ and $c = -3$.

$$b^2 - 4ac = p^2 - 4 \times 2 \times (-3)$$
$$= p^2 + 24.$$

But $p^2 \geqslant 0$ for all p, so $p^2 + 24 > 0$ for all p.

Hence the equation has real (and distinct) roots for all p.

3

See **Differentiation** §5

a

$$y = 6x^2 - x^3$$
$$\frac{dy}{dx} = 12x - 3x^2$$

Remember:
$$\frac{dy}{dx} = m_{tangent}$$

Since the tangent at P has gradient 12:

$$12x - 3x^2 = 12$$
$$3x^2 - 12x + 12 = 0$$
$$x^2 - 4x + 4 = 0$$
$$(x-2)^2 = 0$$
$$x = 2.$$

b When $x = 2$, $y = 6 \times 2^2 - 2^3 = 24 - 8 = 16$. So P is $(2, 16)$.

The equation of the tangent is
$$y - 16 = 12(x-2)$$
$$y - 16 = 12x - 24$$
$$12x - y - 8 = 0.$$

SQP 2

4

See **Wave Functions** §5

a

$$3\cos x° + 5\sin x° = k\cos(x° - a°)$$
$$= k\cos x° \cos a° + k\sin x° \sin a°.$$
$$= (k\cos a°)\cos x° + (k\sin a°)\sin x°.$$

Comparing coefficients:
$$k\sin a° = 5$$
$$k\cos a° = 3$$

$$\frac{\checkmark_S | A \checkmark\checkmark}{T | C \checkmark}$$

So $k = \sqrt{5^2 + 3^2}$ and $\tan a° = \frac{k\sin a°}{k\cos a°} = \frac{5}{3}$
$$= \sqrt{25 + 9}$$
$$= \sqrt{34}$$
$$a = \tan^{-1}\left(\frac{5}{3}\right) = 59 \cdot 04 \text{ (to 2 d.p.)}$$

So $3\cos x° + 5\sin x° = \sqrt{34}\cos(x° - 59 \cdot 04°)$.

cont...

b $3\cos x° + 5\sin x° = 4$ $\qquad 0 \leqslant x \leqslant 90$

$\sqrt{34}\cos(x° - 59·04°) = 4$ $\qquad -59·04 \leqslant x-59·04 \leqslant 30·96.^*$

$\cos(x° - 59·04°) = \dfrac{4}{\sqrt{34}}$

$a = \cos^{-1}\left(\dfrac{4}{\sqrt{34}}\right)$

$\qquad = 46·69 \ (2\,\text{d.p.})$

$x - 59·04 = 46·69 \quad \text{or} \quad 360 - 46·69$

$\qquad\qquad = \cancel{46·69} \quad \text{or} \quad \cancel{313·31}$
$\qquad\qquad\qquad\quad \text{too large (see }^*)$

Look 360° backwards:

$x - 59·04 = 46·69 - 360 \quad \text{or} \quad 313·31 - 360$

$\qquad\qquad = -\cancel{313·31} \quad \text{or} \quad -46·69$
$\qquad\qquad\qquad \text{too small}$

So $\quad x = -46·69 + 59·04$

$\qquad\qquad = 12·35.$

5

See **Differentiation** §11

a

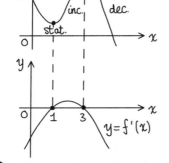

dec: $f(x)$ is decreasing
so $f'(x) < 0$, i.e.
$f'(x)$ is below the x-axis.

inc: $f(x)$ is increasing
so $f'(x) > 0$, i.e.
$f'(x)$ is above the x-axis.

stat: $f(x)$ is stationary
so $f'(x) = 0$, i.e.
$f'(x)$ lies on the x-axis.

SQP 2

6

(a) See **Circles** §6 or §5
(b) See **Circles** §5
(c) See **Straight Lines** §1

a Method 1

The centre is $A(6, 1)$.

$$m_{AP} = \frac{-1-1}{5-6} = \frac{-2}{-1} = 2.$$

> Using:
> $x^2 + y^2 + 2gx + 2fy + c = 0$
> has centre $(-g, -f)$.

So $m_{PT} = -\frac{1}{2}$ since the radius and tangent are perpendicular.

The equation of PT is:

$$y + 1 = -\frac{1}{2}(x - 5) \qquad \text{using point } P(5, -1).$$
$$2y + 2 = -(x - 5) \qquad \text{multiplying by 2.}$$
$$2y + 2 = -x + 5$$
$$x + 2y = 3.$$

Method 2 Write $x + 2y = 3$ as $x = 3 - 2y$ and substitute into the equation of the circle:

$$(3 - 2y)^2 + y^2 - 12(3 - 2y) - 2y + 32 = 0$$
$$9 - 12y + 4y^2 + y^2 - 36 + 24y - 2y + 32 = 0$$
$$5y^2 + 10y + 5 = 0$$
$$y^2 + 2y + 1 = 0$$
$$(y + 1)^2 = 0.$$

Since there is only one solution, the line is a tangent. Check that P lies on the line: $x = 3 - 2 \times (-1) = 5.$

cont...

SQP 2

b Line PT has equation $x = 3 - 2y$. To find points of intersection, substitute this into the equation of the circle:

$$(3 - 2y)^2 + y^2 + 10(3 - 2y) + 2y + 6 = 0$$
$$9 - 12y + 4y^2 + y^2 + 30 - 20y + 2y + 6 = 0$$
$$5y^2 - 30y + 45 = 0$$
$$y^2 - 6y + 9 = 0$$
$$(y - 3)^2 = 0$$
$$y = 3$$

> You could also use the discriminant to show there is just one solution.

Since there is only one solution, the line is a tangent.

c When $y = 3$, $x = 3 - 2 \times 3 = -3$. So Q is the point $(-3, 3)$.

$$\text{So } PQ = \sqrt{(-3 - 5)^2 + (3 - (-1))^2}$$
$$= \sqrt{64 + 16}$$
$$= \sqrt{80}$$
$$= 4\sqrt{5}$$

SQP 2

7

See **Differentiation** §12

a We are told that the surface area is 12 square units.

The surface area is given by:

$$2 \times \text{short side} + 2 \times \text{long side} + \text{base}$$
$$= 2 \times 2x \times h + 2 \times x \times h + 2x \times x$$
$$= 6xh + 2x^2 = 12$$

So
$$6xh = 12 - 2x^2$$
$$3xh = 6 - x^2$$
$$h = \frac{6 - x^2}{3x}.$$

The volume is $V(x) = 2x \times x \times h = 2x^2 \cdot \dfrac{6 - x^2}{3x} = \dfrac{2}{3}x(6 - x^2).$

cont...

b Stationary values exist where $V'(x) = 0$.

$$V(x) = \frac{2}{3}x(6 - x^2) = 4x - \frac{2}{3}x^3.$$

$$V'(x) = 4 - 2x^2 = 0$$
$$2x^2 = 4$$
$$x^2 = 2$$
$$x = \sqrt{2} \quad (\text{no "}\pm\text{" since lengths are positive})$$

Check this gives a maximum...

x	$\sqrt{2}^-$	$\sqrt{2}$	$\sqrt{2}^+$
$V'(x)$	$+$	0	$-$
Sketch	$\diagup$	$-$	$\diagdown$

Hence the maximum volume occurs when $x = \sqrt{2}$.

SQP 2

8

See **Exponentials and Logarithms** §5

a We are told that $A_{1000} = 600$, i.e:

$$A_0 e^{-0.002 \times 1000} = 600$$
$$A_0 e^{-2} = 600$$
$$A_0 = \frac{600}{e^{-2}}$$
$$= 600e^2$$
$$= 4433.43 \text{ micrograms (to 2 d.p.)} \quad \boxed{cont...}$$

b

$$A_t = \tfrac{1}{2} A_0$$

$$A_0 e^{-0.002t} = \tfrac{1}{2} A_0$$

$$e^{-0.002t} = \tfrac{1}{2}$$

$$\log_e e^{-0.002t} = \log_e \tfrac{1}{2} \qquad \text{(taking } \log_e \text{ on both sides)}$$

$$-0.002t = \log_e \tfrac{1}{2}$$

$$t = -\frac{\log_e \tfrac{1}{2}}{0.002}$$

Remember:
- $\log_a x^k = k\log_a x$
- $\log_a a = 1$.

$$= 346.57 \text{ years (to 2 d.p.)}$$

SQP 2

9

See **Integration** §6

To find the limits of integration...

$$2x - \tfrac{1}{2} x^2 = 1.5$$

$$4x - x^2 = 3 \qquad \text{multiplying through by 2.}$$

$$x^2 - 4x + 3 = 0$$

$$(x-1)(x-3) = 0$$

$$x = 1 \quad \text{or} \quad x = 3.$$

The shaded area is given by:

$$\int_1^3 (\text{upper} - \text{lower})\, dx = \int_1^3 \left(2x - \tfrac{1}{2} x^2 - 1.5\right) dx$$

$$= \left[x^2 - \tfrac{1}{6} x^3 - 1.5x\right]_1^3$$

$$= 9 - \tfrac{27}{6} - 4.5 - \left(1 - \tfrac{1}{6} - 1.5\right)$$

$$= \tfrac{2}{3} \text{ square units.}$$

1

See **Sequences** §2

$u_2 = 3u_1 + 4 = 3 \times 2 + 4 = 10.$
$u_3 = 3u_2 + 4 = 3 \times 10 + 4 = 34.$

A

2

See **Circles** §3

Comparing with $x^2 + y^2 + 2gx + 2fy + c$,

$2g = 8$, $2f = 6$ and $c = -75$

$g = 4$ $f = 3$

The circle $x^2 + y^2 + 2gx + 2fy + c = 0$ has radius $\sqrt{g^2 + f^2 - c}$.

The radius is $\sqrt{4^2 + 3^2 + 75} = \sqrt{16 + 9 + 75} = \sqrt{100} = 10.$

B

3

See **Straight Lines** §7

$S = \text{midpoint}_{QR} = \left(\dfrac{3-1}{2}, \dfrac{6-(-4)}{2} \right) = (1, 5).$

So $m_{PS} = \dfrac{5-(-2)}{1-(-3)} = \dfrac{7}{4}.$

D

4

See **Differentiation** §5

$\dfrac{dy}{dx} = 15x^2 - 12.$

Remember: the derivative gives the gradient of the tangent.

When $x = 1$, the gradient of the tangent is $15 \times 1^2 - 12 = 3$ C

5

See **Straight Lines** §1 and §3

The length of ST is $\sqrt{(5-2)^2 + (-1-3)^2} = \sqrt{3^2 + 4^2} = 5$ units

$m_{ST} = \dfrac{-1-3}{5-2} = -\dfrac{4}{3}.$

B

2009

6

See **Sequences** §4

Method 1 $l = \dfrac{b}{1-a}$ with $a = 0.7$ and $b = 10$.

$$l = \frac{10}{1-0.7} = \frac{10}{0.3} = \frac{100}{3}.$$

Method 2   As $n \to \infty$, $u_{n+1} = u_n = l$

So $l = 0.7l + 10$

$0.3l = 10$

$l = \dfrac{10}{0.3} = \dfrac{100}{3}.$

A

7

See **Trigonometry** §4

$$\begin{aligned}
\cos 2x &= 2\cos^2 x - 1 \\
&= 2\left(\frac{1}{\sqrt{5}}\right)^2 - 1 \\
&= \frac{2}{5} - 1 \\
&= -\frac{3}{5}.
\end{aligned}$$

Using:
$\cos 2A = 2\cos^2 A - 1$

A

8

See **Differentiation** §2

$$\frac{1}{4x^3} = \frac{1}{4}x^{-3}.$$

So $\dfrac{d}{dx}\left(\dfrac{1}{4x^3}\right) = \dfrac{d}{dx}\left(\dfrac{1}{4}x^{-3}\right) = -\dfrac{3}{4}x^{-4} = -\dfrac{3}{4x^4}.$

D

9

See **Circles** §4

Put $y = 2x$ in the equation of the circle:

$$\begin{aligned}
x^2 + (2x)^2 &= 5 \\
x^2 + 4x^2 &= 5 \\
5x^2 &= 5 \\
x^2 &= 1 \\
x &= \pm 1.
\end{aligned}$$

A

10

See **Functions and Graphs** §6 and §10
or **Exponentials and Logarithms** §7

Method 1   The curve $y = \log_5 x$ has graph

and $y = \log_5(x-2)$ is this shifted 2 units to the right.

Method 2   When $y = 0$, $\log_5(x-2) = 0$

$$x - 2 = 5^0$$
$$x = 3.$$

So the curve passes through $(3,0)$.

B

11

See **Trigonometry** §1

$(4\sin x - \sqrt{5})(\sin x + 1) = 0$

$4\sin x - \sqrt{5} = 0$ or $\sin x + 1 = 0$

$\sin x = \dfrac{\sqrt{5}}{4}$ $\sin x = -1$

One solution

$y = \sin x$

Since $\dfrac{\sqrt{5}}{4} < 1$ this part has two solutions in $0 \le x < 2\pi$

Therefore there are 3 solutions in $0 \le x < 2\pi$.

B

2009

12

See **Polynomials and Quadratics** §2

Let $a = 2$, $b = -1$ and $c = -9$, then the discriminant is

$$b^2 - 4ac = (-1)^2 - 4 \times 2 \times (-9) = 1 + 72 = 73.$$

Since $b^2 - 4ac > 0$, the roots are real and distinct, and because 73 is not a square number, the roots are not rational.

C

13

See **Wave Functions** §1

$k\sin a° = 1$
$k\cos a° = \sqrt{3}$

$$\frac{\;S\;|\;A\;}{\;T\;|\;C\;}$$ ✓✓ ✓ ✓

So $k = \sqrt{1^2 + \sqrt{3}^2}$
$= \sqrt{4}$
$= 2$

and $\tan a° = \dfrac{k\sin a°}{k\cos a°} = \dfrac{1}{\sqrt{3}}$

$a = \tan^{-1}\left(\dfrac{1}{\sqrt{3}}\right)$
$= 30.$

Exact value...

B

14

See **Functions and Graphs** §9 and §10

$$f(x) = 2\sin\left(3x - \tfrac{\pi}{2}\right) + 5$$

Scales the graph to have amplitude 2

Shifts the graph 5 units up the y-axis.

So the range is $3 \le f(x) \le 7$.

C

15

See **Straight Lines** §3

The line makes an angle of $\dfrac{\pi}{2} - \dfrac{\pi}{6} = \dfrac{\pi}{3}$ with the positive direction of the x-axis.

So the gradient is $\tan\dfrac{\pi}{3} = \sqrt{3}$.

Exact value...

A

16

See **Integration** §5

Since the shaded region lies below the x-axis, its area is given by

$$-\int_0^1 (4x^3 - 9x^2)\, dx = -\left[x^4 - 3x^3\right]_0^1.$$

B

17   *See **Vectors** §3*

$$|\underline{u}| = \sqrt{(-3)^2 + 4^2} = \sqrt{25} = 5.$$

So $\frac{1}{5}\underline{u}$ is a unit vector parallel to $\underline{u}$.

$$\frac{1}{5}\underline{u} = \begin{pmatrix} -3/5 \\ 0 \\ 4/5 \end{pmatrix} = -\frac{3}{5}\underline{i} + \frac{4}{5}\underline{k}.$$

A

18   *See **Further Calculus** §4*

Using the chain rule,
$$f'(x) = -\frac{1}{2}\left(4 - 3x^2\right)^{-3/2} \times \frac{d}{dx}\left(4 - 3x^2\right)$$
$$= -\frac{1}{2}\left(4 - 3x^2\right)^{-3/2} \times (-6x)$$
$$= 3x\left(4 - 3x^2\right)^{-3/2}.$$

D

19   *See **Polynomials and Quadratics** §6*

$$6 + x - x^2 < 0$$
$$-\left(x^2 - x - 6\right) < 0$$
$$-\left(x + 2\right)\left(x - 3\right) < 0$$

From the sketch, $x < -2$ or $x > 3$.

Sketch:

From the sketch, $x < -2$ or $x > 3$.

C

20   *See **Differentiation** §4*

$$\frac{dA}{dr} = 4\pi r + 6\pi.$$

When $r = 2$, $\frac{dA}{dr} = 8\pi + 6\pi = 14\pi$.

Remember:
"rate of change"
means "derivative".

C

21

*See **Straight Lines** – (a) §6, (b) §8, (c) §6 and §10*

a Put $y = 0$ in the equation of PQ:

$$6x - 7 \times 0 + 18 = 0$$
$$6x = -18$$
$$x = -3. \quad \text{So } P \text{ has coordinates } (-3, 0).$$

b $m_{QR} = \dfrac{-2-6}{8-4} = \dfrac{-8}{4} = -2.$ So $m_{alt.} = \dfrac{1}{2}$ since $m_{QR} \times m_{alt.} = -1.$

So the equation is $\quad y = \dfrac{1}{2}(x+3) \quad$ using point $P(-3, 0)$

$$2y = x + 3$$

c We know $m_{QR} = -2.$

So the equation of QR is $\quad y - 6 = -2(x - 4) \quad$ using point $Q(4, 6)$.
$$y - 6 = -2x + 8$$
$$y = -2x + 14.$$

Solve the equations of QR and PT simultaneously...

$$2y = x + 3 \quad\text{———}\quad ①$$
$$y = -2x + 14 \quad\text{——}\quad ②$$

$② + 2 \times ①: \quad 5y = 20$
$$y = 4$$

When $y = 4, \quad x = 2 \times 4 - 3 = 5.$ So T is the point $(5, 4)$.

22

See **Vectors** – (a) §9 and §10, (b) §13

a i

$$\overrightarrow{DE} = \underline{e} - \underline{d} = \begin{pmatrix} 1 \\ -2 \\ -3 \end{pmatrix} - \begin{pmatrix} 10 \\ -8 \\ -15 \end{pmatrix} = \begin{pmatrix} -9 \\ 6 \\ 12 \end{pmatrix} = 3\begin{pmatrix} -3 \\ 2 \\ 4 \end{pmatrix}$$

$$\overrightarrow{EF} = \underline{f} - \underline{e} = \begin{pmatrix} -2 \\ 0 \\ 1 \end{pmatrix} - \begin{pmatrix} 1 \\ -2 \\ -3 \end{pmatrix} = \begin{pmatrix} -3 \\ 2 \\ 4 \end{pmatrix}$$

$\overrightarrow{EF}$ and $\overrightarrow{DE}$ have a common point and, since $3\overrightarrow{EF} = \overrightarrow{DE}$, they have a common direction. Hence D, E and F are collinear.

ii Since $3\overrightarrow{EF} = \overrightarrow{DE}$, E divides DF in the ratio 3:1.

b

$$\overrightarrow{GE} = \underline{e} - \underline{g} = \begin{pmatrix} 1 \\ -2 \\ -3 \end{pmatrix} - \begin{pmatrix} k \\ 1 \\ 0 \end{pmatrix} = \begin{pmatrix} 1-k \\ -3 \\ -3 \end{pmatrix}.$$

Since DE and GE are perpendicular, $\overrightarrow{DE} . \overrightarrow{GE} = 0$. So

$$-9(1-k) + 6 \times (-3) + 12 \times (-3) = 0$$
$$-9 + 9k - 18 - 36 = 0$$
$$9k = 63$$
$$k = 7.$$

23

See **Functions and Graphs** §10

a

$y = f(2x)$ multiplies each x-coordinate by $\frac{1}{2}$.

b $y = 1 - f(2x) = -f(2x) + 1$.

24

See **Trigonometry** §3

a $\sin\left(\dfrac{7\pi}{12}\right) = \sin\left(\dfrac{\pi}{3}+\dfrac{\pi}{4}\right) = \sin\dfrac{\pi}{3}\cos\dfrac{\pi}{4}+\cos\dfrac{\pi}{3}\sin\dfrac{\pi}{4}$

$\qquad\qquad\qquad = \dfrac{\sqrt{3}}{2}\times\dfrac{1}{\sqrt{2}}+\dfrac{1}{2}\times\dfrac{1}{\sqrt{2}}$

$\qquad\qquad\qquad = \dfrac{\sqrt{3}+1}{2\sqrt{2}}$

Using:
$\sin(A+B)$
$= \sin A\cos B + \cos A \sin B$

b $\sin(A+B) = \sin A\cos B + \cos A\sin B$

$\sin(A-B) = \sin A\cos B - \cos A\sin B$

Adding gives $\sin(A+B) + \sin(A-B) = 2\sin A\cos B.$

c **i** $\dfrac{\pi}{12} = \dfrac{\pi}{3} - \dfrac{\pi}{4}$

ii Since $\dfrac{7\pi}{12} = \dfrac{\pi}{3}+\dfrac{\pi}{4}$ and $\dfrac{\pi}{12} = \dfrac{\pi}{3}-\dfrac{\pi}{4}$, use the above formula

with $A = \dfrac{\pi}{3}$ and $B = \dfrac{\pi}{4}$.

$\sin\left(\dfrac{7\pi}{12}\right) + \sin\left(\dfrac{\pi}{12}\right) = 2\sin\dfrac{\pi}{3}\cos\dfrac{\pi}{4}$

$\qquad\qquad\qquad = 2\times\dfrac{\sqrt{3}}{2}\times\dfrac{1}{\sqrt{2}}$

$\qquad\qquad\qquad = \dfrac{\sqrt{3}}{\sqrt{2}} = \dfrac{\sqrt{6}}{2}$

Exact values...

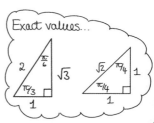

1

See **Differentiation** §7 and §8

Stationary points exist where $\frac{dy}{dx} = 0$.

$$\frac{dy}{dx} = 3x^2 - 6x - 9 = 0$$
$$3(x^2 - 2x - 3) = 0$$
$$(x + 1)(x - 3) = 0$$
$$x = -1, \quad x = 3.$$

When $x = -1$, $y = (-1)^3 - 3 \times (-1)^2 - 9 \times (-1) + 12$
$$= -1 - 3 + 9 + 12$$
$$= 17. \qquad (-1, 17).$$

When $x = 3$, $y = 3^3 - 3 \times 3^2 - 9 \times 3 + 12$
$$= -15. \qquad (3, -15).$$

Method 1   Nature table:

x	-1^-	-1	-1^+	3^-	3	3^+
dy/dx	+	0	−	−	0	+
Sketch	/	—	\	\	_	/

Method 2   Second derivative test: $\frac{d^2y}{dx^2} = 6x - 6$.

When $x = -1$, $\frac{d^2y}{dx^2} = 6 \times (-1) - 6 = -12 < 0$

When $x = 3$, $\frac{d^2y}{dx^2} = 6 \times 3 - 6 = 12 > 0$.

So $(-1, 17)$ is a maximum turning point.
$(3, -15)$ is a minimum turning point.

2

(a) See **Functions and Graphs** §3
(b) See **Differentiation** §2

a **i** $p(x) = f(g(x)) = f(x^2-2) = 3(x^2-2)+1 = 3x^2-5.$

ii $q(x) = g(f(x)) = g(3x+1) = (3x+1)^2-2.$

b $p'(x) = 6x$ and $q'(x) = 2(3x+1) \times \dfrac{d}{dx}(3x+1) = 6(3x+1).$

So $6x = 6(3x+1)$

$x = 3x+1$

$2x = -1$

$x = -\dfrac{1}{2}.$

3

(a) See **Polynomials and Quadratics** §9
(b) See **Exponentials and Logarithms** §3 and §5

a **i** <u>**Method 1**</u> Put $x=1$ in the left-hand side:

$$1^3 + 8 \times 1^2 + 11 \times 1 - 20 = 1+8+11-20 = 0.$$

So $x=1$ is a root of the equation.

<u>**Method 2**</u> Using synthetic division...

$$\begin{array}{r|rrrr} 1 & 1 & 8 & 11 & -20 \\ & & 1 & 9 & 20 \\ \hline & 1 & 9 & 20 & \boxed{0} \end{array}$$

Since the remainder is 0,
$x=1$ is a root.

ii $x^3 + 8x^2 + 11x - 20 = (x-1)(x^2+9x+20)$ ← By inspection or from the table.

$\qquad\qquad\qquad\qquad\quad = (x-1)(x+4)(x+5).$

cont...

2009

b

$$\log_2(x+3) + \log_2(x^2+5x-4) = 3$$
$$\log_2\left((x+3)(x^2+5x-4)\right) = 3$$
$$(x+3)(x^2+5x-4) = 2^3$$
$$x^3 + 8x^2 + 11x - 12 = 8$$
$$x^3 + 8x^2 + 11x - 20 = 0$$
$$(x-1)(x+4)(x+5) = 0$$

So $x=1$, $x=-4$, $x=-5$

> Remember:
> • $\log_a x + \log_a y = \log_a xy$
> • $\log_a x = y \Leftrightarrow x = a^y$

> Remember: we can only take log of a positive number.

But when $x=-4$, $\log_2(x+3) = \log_2(-1)$ which is undefined.

$x=-5$, $\log_2(x+3) = \log_2(-2)$ which is undefined.

So the only solution is $x=1$.

4

> (a) See **Circles** §2
> (b) See **Straight Lines** §2 and **Circles** §6
> (c) See **Circles** §7

a Put $x=5$ and $y=10$ in the left-hand side:

$$(5+1)^2 + (10-2)^2 = 36 + 64 = 100.$$

Since this equals the right-hand side, P lies on the circle.

b The circle has centre $C(-1, 2)$.

> The circle $(x-a)^2 + (y-b)^2 = r^2$ has centre (a, b).

Let Q have coordinates (x_Q, y_Q). Since C is the midpoint of PQ,

$$(-1, 2) = \left(\frac{x_Q + 5}{2}, \frac{y_Q + 10}{2}\right).$$

So $x_Q + 5 = -2$ and $y_Q + 10 = 4$
$$x_Q = -7 \qquad y_Q = -6.$$

Hence Q is the point $(-7, -6)$.

Now $m_{PQ} = m_{CP} = \dfrac{10-2}{5-(-1)} = \dfrac{8}{6} = \dfrac{4}{3}$,

so $m_{tgt.} = -\dfrac{3}{4}$ since $m_{PQ} \times m_{tgt.} = -1$.

cont...

2009

Therefore the equation of the tangent at Q is

$$y + 6 = -\frac{3}{4}(x+7) \qquad \text{using } Q(-7,-6).$$
$$4y + 24 = -3x - 21$$
$$3x + 4y + 45 = 0.$$

c Circle C_1 has radius 10.
So the radii of C_2 and C_3 are both 20.

> The circle $(x-a)^2 + (y-b)^2 = r^2$ has radius r.

The point $P(5,10)$ is the centre of C_2, so the equation of C_2 is

Sketch:

$$(x-5)^2 + (y-10)^2 = 20^2$$
i.e. $(x-5)^2 + (y-10)^2 = 400.$

The point Q is the midpoint of PR, so

$$\left(\frac{5+x_R}{2}, \frac{10+y_R}{2}\right) = (-7,-6)$$

i.e. $\dfrac{5+x_R}{2} = -7 \qquad$ and $\qquad \dfrac{10+y_R}{2} = -6$
$$x_R = -19. \qquad\qquad\qquad y_R = -22.$$

So R is the point $(-19,-22)$ and C_3 has equation

$$(x+19)^2 + (y+22)^2 = 400.$$

5

(a) See **Functions and Graphs** §9
(b) See **Trigonometry** §1
(c) See **Integration** §6

a The period of $g(x)$ is π, so $n = 2$. The amplitude is 3 so $m = 3$.

b The curves intersect where

$$-4\cos 2x + 3 = 3\cos 2x$$
$$7\cos 2x = 3$$
$$\cos 2x = \frac{3}{7}.$$

$$\begin{array}{c|c}
\pi - a & a \\
\hline
S & A \checkmark \\
\hline
T & C \checkmark \\
\hline
\pi + a & 2\pi - a
\end{array}$$

$$a = \cos^{-1}\left(\frac{3}{7}\right)$$
$$= 1.128 \quad (\text{to 3 d.p.})$$

So $2x = 1.128$ or $2x = 2\pi - 1.128$
$\quad x = 0.564 \qquad x = 2.578 \quad (\text{to 3 d.p.})$

When $x = 0.564$, $y = 3\cos(2 \times 0.564)$
$$= 1.285.$$

> To get a more accurate answer, we can work to 3 d.p. and round at the end.

When $x = 2.578$, $y = 3\cos(2 \times 2.578)$
$$= 1.288. \quad (\text{both to 3 d.p.})$$

So the points of intersection are $(0.6, 1.3)$ and $(2.6, 1.3)$ to 1 d.p.

c The shaded area is

$$\int_{0.6}^{2.6} (\text{upper} - \text{lower})\, dx$$

$$= \int_{0.6}^{2.6} \left(-4\cos 2x + 3 - 3\cos 2x\right) dx$$

$$= \int_{0.6}^{2.6} \left(-7\cos 2x + 3\right) dx$$

$$= \left[-\frac{7}{2}\sin 2x + 3x\right]_{0.6}^{2.6}$$

> Using:
> $$\int \cos ax \, dx = \frac{1}{a}\sin ax + c.$$

$$= 10.89 + 1.46$$

$$= 12.4 \quad \text{square units} \quad (\text{to 1 d.p.})$$

6

See **Exponentials and Logarithms** §5

a Let N be the population in millions.

- The rate of increase is $1.6\% = 0.016$. So $r = 0.016$.
- 2020 is 14 years after 2006, so $t = 14$.

$N = N_0 e^{rt} = 61 e^{0.016 \times 14} = 76.32$ (to 2 d.p.)

So the population would be 76.32 million.

b This time, $r = 0.43\% = 0.0043$.

For the population to double, $N = 2N_0$ so

$$N = N_0 e^{0.0043t}$$
$$2N_0 = N_0 e^{0.0043t}$$
$$e^{0.0043t} = 2$$
$$0.0043t = \log_e 2$$

Remember:
$$a^y = x \Leftrightarrow y = \log_a x$$

$$t = \frac{\log_e 2}{0.0043}$$

$$t = 161.20 \text{ (to 2 d.p.)}$$

So the population would take 161.20 years to double.

7

See **Vectors** – (a) §14 and §11, (b) §5 and §3

a

$$\underline{p} \cdot (\underline{q} + \underline{r}) = \underline{p} \cdot \underline{q} + \underline{p} \cdot \underline{r}$$

$$= |\underline{p}||\underline{q}|\cos 30° + 0 \quad \longleftarrow \text{ since } \underline{p} \text{ and } \underline{r} \text{ are perpendicular.}$$

$$= 4 \times 3 \times \cos 30°$$

$$= 4 \times 3 \times \frac{\sqrt{3}}{2}$$

$$= 6\sqrt{3}.$$

Exact values...

$$\underline{r} \cdot (\underline{p} - \underline{q}) = \underline{r} \cdot \underline{p} - \underline{r} \cdot \underline{q}$$

$$= 0 - |\underline{r}||\underline{q}|\cos\theta$$

$$= -\frac{3}{2} \times 3 \times (-\cos 60°)$$

$$= \frac{3}{2} \times 3 \times \frac{1}{2}$$

$$= \frac{9}{4}.$$

$\theta = 60°$

$$|\underline{r}| = 3\sin 30° = \frac{3}{2}.$$

b

From the diagram, $\underline{q} + \underline{r} = \overrightarrow{DE}$

and $\underline{p} - \underline{q} = -\underline{q} + \underline{p} = \overrightarrow{AC}$

Using Pythagoras's theorem:

$$|\underline{q} + \underline{r}| = \sqrt{3^2 - (3/2)^2} = \sqrt{\frac{27}{4}} = \frac{\sqrt{9}\sqrt{3}}{\sqrt{4}} = \frac{3\sqrt{3}}{2} \quad \left(= 2.60 \text{ to 2 d.p.} \right)$$

Now $|EC| = |\underline{p}| - \frac{3\sqrt{3}}{2} = 4 - \frac{3\sqrt{3}}{2}$

So $|\underline{p} - \underline{q}| = \sqrt{\left(4 - \frac{3\sqrt{3}}{2}\right)^2 + \left(\frac{3}{2}\right)^2} = \sqrt{25 - 12\sqrt{3}} \quad \left(= 2.05 \text{ to 2 d.p.} \right)$

2009

87

1

See **Straight Lines** §5 and §6

To extract the gradient, rearrange to give $y = mx + c \ldots$

$$2x - 3y - 6 = 0$$
$$3y = 2x - 6$$
$$y = \frac{2}{3}x - 2$$

So this line has gradient $\frac{2}{3}$.

Therefore L has gradient $-\frac{3}{2}$ since $m \times m_\perp = -1$. **A**

2

See **Sequences** §2

$$u_1 = 2u_0 + 3 = 2 \times 1 + 3 = 5$$
$$u_2 = 2u_1 + 3 = 2 \times 5 + 3 = 13$$

C

3

See **Vectors** §5 and §6

$$3\underline{u} - 2\underline{v} = 3\begin{pmatrix} 2 \\ 0 \\ 1 \end{pmatrix} - 2\begin{pmatrix} -1 \\ 2 \\ 4 \end{pmatrix} = \begin{pmatrix} 6 \\ 0 \\ 3 \end{pmatrix} - \begin{pmatrix} -2 \\ 4 \\ 8 \end{pmatrix} = \begin{pmatrix} 8 \\ -4 \\ -5 \end{pmatrix}$$

D

4

See **Functions and Graphs** §9 and §10

The amplitude (height) is 2 so $a = 2$.

The period is $\frac{2\pi}{3}$ so $b = 3$. **A**

5

Method 1 Compensating...

See **Polynomials and Quadratics** §3

$$x^2 + 8x + 3 = (x+4)^2 - 16 + 3 = (x+4)^2 - 13. \text{ So } q = -13.$$

This gives the correct x^2 and x terms, and an extra 16

Take off this extra 16

cont...

2010

89

Method 2   Comparing coefficients...

$$x^2 + 8x + 3 = (x+p)^2 + q$$
$$= x^2 + 2px + p^2 + q.$$

So $2p = 8$ and $p^2 + q = 3$
     $p = 4$ $q = 3 - 16$
                         $= -13.$

B

6

See **Polynomials and Quadratics** §2

Given $kx^2 - 3x + 2 = 0$, let $a = k$, $b = -3$ and $c = 2$.

For equal roots, $b^2 - 4ac = 0$ i.e.

$$(-3)^2 - 4 \times k \times 2 = 0$$
$$8k = 9$$
$$k = \frac{9}{8}.$$

D

7

See **Sequences** §4

Method 1 $l = \dfrac{b}{1-a}$ with $a = \frac{1}{4}$ and $b = 7$.

$$l = \frac{7}{1 - \frac{1}{4}} = \frac{7}{3/4} = \frac{28}{3}.$$

Method 2   As $n \to \infty$, $u_{n+1} = u_n = l$

So $l = \frac{1}{4} l + 7$
     $\frac{3}{4} l = 7$
     $l = \frac{28}{3}.$

C

8

See **Circles** §3

Comparing with $x^2 + y^2 + 2gx + 2fy + c$,

$2g = -6$ $2f = -10$ and $c = 9$
$g = -3$ $f = -5$

The circle
$x^2 + y^2 + 2gx + 2fy + c = 0$
has centre $(-g, -f)$.

The centre is $(3, 5)$. So l has equation $y = 10$.

B

9 $\int \left(2x^{-4} + \cos 5x \right) dx$

See **Integration** §1 and **Further Calculus** §2

$= \dfrac{2x^{-3}}{-3} + \dfrac{1}{5} \sin 5x + c$

Using:
$\int \cos ax \, dx = \dfrac{1}{a} \sin ax + c.$

$= -\dfrac{2}{3} x^{-3} + \dfrac{1}{5} \sin 5x + c.$

C

10

See **Vectors** §13

The vectors are perpendicular $\Leftrightarrow$ their scalar product is zero.

$\left(x\underline{i} + 5\underline{j} + 7\underline{k} \right) . \left(-3\underline{i} + 2\underline{j} - \underline{k} \right) = 0$

$x \times (-3) + 5 \times 2 + 7 \times (-1) = 0$

$-3x + 3 = 0$

$x = 1.$

B

11

See **Functions and Graphs** §3 and §8

$f\left(g\left(\tfrac{\pi}{6} \right) \right) = f\left(\tfrac{\pi}{6} + \tfrac{\pi}{6} \right)$

$= f\left(\tfrac{\pi}{3} \right)$

$= \cos \tfrac{\pi}{3}$

$= \dfrac{1}{2}.$

Exact values...

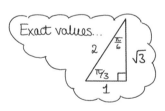

D

12

See **Differentiation** §2

$f(x) = x^{-1/5}.$ So $f'(x) = -\dfrac{1}{5} x^{-6/5}.$

A

2010

13

See **Polynomials and Quadratics** §1 and §2

- $a > 0$ means the parabola is concave up $(\cup\text{-shaped})$
- $b^2 - 4ac > 0$ means the parabola intersects the x-axis at two distinct points.

B

14

See **Integration** §6

The shaded area between $x = -2$ and $x = 2$ is given by

$$\int_{-2}^{2} (\text{upper} - \text{lower})\, dx = \int_{-2}^{2} \left(14 - x^2 - (2x^2 + 2)\right) dx$$
$$= \int_{-2}^{2} \left(12 - 3x^2\right) dx$$

C

15

See **Differentiation** §6 and §7

At $x = 1$, $f'(1) = 1^2 - 9 = -8 < 0$. So the function is decreasing.
At $x = -3$, $f'(-3) = (-3)^2 - 9 = 0$. So the function is stationary.

C

16

See **Polynomials and Quadratics** §12

The curve intersects the x-axis where
$$k(x-1)^2(x+t) = 0.$$
i.e. $x = 1$ and $x = -t$.

Hence $-t = 5$ i.e. $t = -5$.
When $x = 0$, $y = k(-1)^2(-5) = 10$. So $k = -2$.

A

17

See **Differentiation** §4

$s(t) = t^2 - 5t + 8$
$s'(t) = 2t - 5$
$s'(3) = 2 \times 3 - 5 = 1.$

Remember:
"rate of change"
means "derivative".

B

18

See **Polynomials and Quadratics** §6

$x^2 + 4x > 0$
$x(x+4) > 0$

From the sketch, $x < -4$ or $x > 0$.

Sketch:

$y = x(x+4)$

B

19

See **Exponentials and Logarithms** §7

The points $(4, 0)$ and $(6, 1)$ both lie on the curve.
So $\log_a(4+b) = 0$ and $\log_a(6+b) = 1.$
  $\log_a(4+b) = 0 \Leftrightarrow a^0 = 4+b$ ie $b = -3$
Then $\log_a 3 = 1 \Leftrightarrow a^1 = 3$ ie $a = 3.$

C

20

See **Functions and Graphs** §10

Method 1 Since $(6, 4)$ lies on $y = f(2x) - 3,$
   $4 = f(2 \times 6) - 3$ ie $f(12) = 7.$
So $y = f(x)$ has turning point $(12, 7).$

Method 2 Points on the curve $y = f(2x) - 3$ are points on
$y = f(x)$ with the x-coordinates halved, and then
shifted down by 3.
So to see where $(6, 4)$ came from, reverse this:
   $(6 \times 2, 4+3) = (12, 7).$

A

2010

21

(a) See **Straight Lines** §7
(b) See **Straight Lines** §6
(c) See **Vectors** §10

a $\text{midpoint}_{AC} = \left(\dfrac{4+18}{2}, \dfrac{0+20}{2} \right) = (11,10)$. So $Q(11,10)$.

$m_{BQ} = \dfrac{10-16}{11-(-4)} = -\dfrac{6}{15} = -\dfrac{2}{5}$

So the equation of BQ is

$$y - 16 = -\frac{2}{5}(x - (-4)) \quad \text{using } B(-4,16)$$
$$5y - 80 = -2x - 8$$
$$2x + 5y - 72 = 0. \quad\text{---} \quad (*)$$

b Put $x = 6$ and $y = 12$ in the LHS of $(*)$:

$$2 \times 6 + 5 \times 12 - 72 = 12 + 60 - 72 = 0 = \text{RHS}$$

So T lies on BQ.

c $\overrightarrow{BT} = \underline{t} - \underline{b} = \begin{pmatrix} 6 \\ 12 \end{pmatrix} - \begin{pmatrix} -4 \\ 16 \end{pmatrix} = \begin{pmatrix} 10 \\ -4 \end{pmatrix} = 2\begin{pmatrix} 5 \\ -2 \end{pmatrix}$.

$\overrightarrow{TQ} = \underline{q} - \underline{t} = \begin{pmatrix} 11 \\ 10 \end{pmatrix} - \begin{pmatrix} 6 \\ 12 \end{pmatrix} = \begin{pmatrix} 5 \\ -2 \end{pmatrix}$

So $2\overrightarrow{TQ} = \overrightarrow{BT}$ ie $\dfrac{BT}{TQ} = \dfrac{2}{1}$

So T divides BQ in the ratio $2:1$.

22

See **Polynomials and Quadratics** – (a) and (b) §9,
(c) and (d) §7 and §11

a i $x - 1$ is a factor $\Leftrightarrow f(1) = 0$.

Method 1 $f(1) = 2 \times 1^3 + 1^2 - 8 \times 1 + 5 = 2 + 1 - 8 + 5 = 0$.

Method 2 Using synthetic division...

$$
\begin{array}{c|cccc}
1 & 2 & 1 & -8 & 5 \\
  &   & 2 & 3 & -5 \\
\hline
  & 2 & 3 & -5 & \boxed{0}
\end{array}
$$

Since $f(1) = 0$, $x - 1$ is a factor of $f(x)$.

ii $\begin{aligned}
f(x) &= 2x^3 + x^2 - 8x + 5 \\
&= (x-1)(2x^2 + 3x - 5) \quad \leftarrow \text{By inspection or from the table.} \\
&= (x-1)(2x+5)(x-1) \\
&= (x-1)^2(2x+5).
\end{aligned}$

b $\begin{aligned}
2x^3 + x^2 - 8x + 5 &= 0 \\
(x-1)^2(2x+5) &= 0 \\
x = 1 \quad &\text{or} \quad x = -\frac{5}{2}
\end{aligned}$

c Equate to find the points of intersection ...

$$
\begin{aligned}
2x^3 + x^2 - 6x + 2 &= 2x - 3 \\
2x^3 + x^2 - 8x + 5 &= 0 \\
(x-1)^2(2x+5) &= 0 \quad \leftarrow \text{From above} \\
x = 1 \quad &\text{or} \quad x = -\frac{5}{2}
\end{aligned}
$$

Since $x = 1$ is a repeated root, the line is a tangent to the curve at the point where $x = 1$.

At $x = 1$, $y = 2 \times 1 - 3 = -1$. So $G(1, -1)$.

d The other point of intersection has $x = -\frac{5}{2}$.

At $x = -\frac{5}{2}$, $y = 2 \times \left(-\frac{5}{2}\right) - 3 = -8$. So $H\left(-\frac{5}{2}, -8\right)$.

2010

23

(a) and (b) See **Straight Lines** §3 and §6, and **Trigonometry** §3
(c) See **Trigonometry** §3

a i To extract the gradient of OA, rearrange to the form $y = mx + c$ ...

$$3x - 2y = 0 \quad \text{i.e.} \quad y = \frac{3}{2}x$$

So the gradient m is $\frac{3}{2}$.

Hence $\tan a = \frac{3}{2}$.

> Remember: the line $y = mx + c$ has $m = \tan \vartheta$ where ϑ is the angle between the line and the positive direction of the x-axis.

ii $\tan a = \frac{\text{opp.}}{\text{adj.}} = \frac{3}{2}$. So we have:

> By Pythagoras's theorem.

So $\sin a = \frac{\text{opp.}}{\text{hyp.}} = \frac{3}{\sqrt{13}}$.

b $3x - 4y = 0 \Leftrightarrow y = \frac{3}{4}x$. So OB has gradient $\frac{3}{4}$.

Hence $\tan b = \frac{3}{4}$, so we have:

> By Pythagoras's theorem.

So $\sin b = \frac{\text{opp.}}{\text{hyp.}} = \frac{3}{5}$ and $\cos b = \frac{\text{adj.}}{\text{hyp.}} = \frac{4}{5}$.

c i $\sin(a - b) = \sin a \cos b - \cos a \sin b$

$$= \frac{3}{\sqrt{13}} \times \frac{4}{5} - \frac{2}{\sqrt{13}} \times \frac{3}{5}$$

$$= \frac{12}{5\sqrt{13}} - \frac{6}{5\sqrt{13}}$$

$$= \frac{6}{5\sqrt{13}}$$

> Using:
> $\sin(A - B)$
> $= \sin A \cos B - \cos A \sin B$

ii $\sin(b - a) = -\sin(-(b-a))$

$$= -\sin(a - b)$$

$$= -\frac{6}{5\sqrt{13}}.$$

> Remember:
> $\sin x = -\sin(-x)$
> (think about the graph)

> You could also use the addition formula again but this is more work.

2010

1

See **Vectors** – (a) and (b) §2, §5 and §6, (c) §12

a From the diagram...
- R has coordinates $(0, 2, 0)$ so M is the point $(0, 1, 0)$.
- N lies ⅔ of the way along $\overrightarrow{QU}$ so N$(4, 2, 2)$.

b Again from the diagram V is the point $(0, 2, 3)$.

$$\overrightarrow{VM} = \underline{m} - \underline{v} = \begin{pmatrix} 0 \\ 1 \\ 0 \end{pmatrix} - \begin{pmatrix} 0 \\ 2 \\ 3 \end{pmatrix} = \begin{pmatrix} 0 \\ -1 \\ -3 \end{pmatrix}$$

$$\overrightarrow{VN} = \underline{n} - \underline{v} = \begin{pmatrix} 4 \\ 2 \\ 2 \end{pmatrix} - \begin{pmatrix} 0 \\ 2 \\ 3 \end{pmatrix} = \begin{pmatrix} 4 \\ 0 \\ -1 \end{pmatrix}$$

c M$\hat{V}$N is the angle between $\overrightarrow{VM}$ and $\overrightarrow{VN}$.

$$|\overrightarrow{VM}| = \sqrt{0^2 + (-1)^2 + (-3)^2} = \sqrt{10}$$
$$|\overrightarrow{VN}| = \sqrt{4^2 + 0^2 + (-1)^2} = \sqrt{17}$$

Method 1

$$\cos M\hat{V}N = \frac{\overrightarrow{VM} \cdot \overrightarrow{VN}}{|\overrightarrow{VM}||\overrightarrow{VN}|}$$

Using:
$$\underline{a} \cdot \underline{b} = |\underline{a}||\underline{b}|\cos\vartheta$$

$$= \frac{0 \times 4 + (-1) \times 0 + (-3) \times (-1)}{\sqrt{10}\sqrt{17}}$$

$$= \frac{3}{\sqrt{10}\sqrt{17}}$$

$$M\hat{V}N = \cos^{-1}\left(\frac{3}{\sqrt{10}\sqrt{17}}\right)$$

$$= 76.70 \text{ (to 2 d.p.)}$$
$$\text{OR } 1.339 \text{ rads (to 3 d.p.)}$$

cont...

2010

Method 2 $|\overrightarrow{MN}| = \left|\begin{pmatrix} 4 \\ 1 \\ 2 \end{pmatrix}\right| = \sqrt{16+1+4} = \sqrt{21}.$

$\cos M\hat{V}N = \dfrac{10+17-21}{2\sqrt{10}\sqrt{17}}$

$= \dfrac{3}{\sqrt{10}\sqrt{17}}$

> Remember the cosine rule:
> $\cos A = \dfrac{b^2+c^2-a^2}{2bc}$

So $M\hat{V}N = 76\cdot70°$ (to 2 d.p.) or $1\cdot339$ rads (to 3 d.p.)

2

See **Wave Functions** – (a) §2, (b) §4

a

$12\cos x° - 5\sin x° = k\cos(x°+a°)$
$= k\cos x°\cos a° - k\sin a°\sin x°$
$= (k\cos a°)\cos x° - (k\sin a°)\sin x°$

Comparing coefficients: $\begin{aligned} k\cos a° &= 12 \\ k\sin a° &= 5 \end{aligned}$

$\dfrac{\checkmark\ S\ \big|\ A\ \checkmark\checkmark}{\ \ \ T\ \big|\ C\ \checkmark}$

So $k = \sqrt{12^2+5^2}$ and $\tan a° = \dfrac{k\sin a°}{k\cos a°} = \dfrac{5}{12}.$
$= \sqrt{169}$
$= 13$

$a = \tan^{-1}\left(\dfrac{5}{12}\right)$
$= 22\cdot62$ (to 2 d.p.)

So $12\cos x° - 5\sin x° = 13\cos(x° + 22\cdot62°).$

b i The maximum value is 13 and the minimum value is -13.

ii The "$+22\cdot62°$" shifts the graph of $y = 13\cos x°$ to the left.

So the maximum occurs at
$x = 360 - 22\cdot62 = 337\cdot38$

and the minimum occurs at
$x = 180 - 22\cdot62 = 157\cdot38$

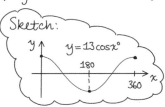

Sketch:

$y = 13\cos x°$

and only at these values in the interval $0 \le x < 360$.

3

(a) See **Circles** §5
(b) See **Circles** §3 and §1, and **Vectors** §10

a **i** Put $y = 3-x$ in the equation of the circle:

$$x^2 + (3-x)^2 + 14x + 4(3-x) - 19 = 0$$
$$x^2 + 9 - 6x + x^2 + 14x + 12 - 4x - 19 = 0$$
$$2x^2 + 4x + 2 = 0$$
$$2(x^2 + 2x + 1) = 0$$
$$(x+1)^2 = 0$$
$$x = -1.$$

> You could also use the discriminant to show there is just one solution

Since there is only one solution, the line is a tangent.

ii When $x = -1$, $y = 3 - (-1) = 4$. So P is the point $(-1, 4)$.

b The larger circle has centre $D(-7, -2)$ and radius $\sqrt{(-7)^2 + (-2)^2 + 19}$
$$= \sqrt{72}$$
$$= 6\sqrt{2} \text{ units.}$$

> The circle
> $x^2 + y^2 + 2gx + 2fy + c = 0$
> has centre $(-g, -f)$ and
> radius $\sqrt{g^2 + f^2 - c}$

So the radius of the smaller circle is $\frac{1}{3} \times 6\sqrt{2} = 2\sqrt{2}$ units.

To find C... $\quad \overrightarrow{DP} = 3\overrightarrow{PC}$
$$\underline{p} - \underline{d} = 3(\underline{c} - \underline{p})$$
$$3\underline{c} = 4\underline{p} - \underline{d}$$
$$= \binom{-4}{16} - \binom{-7}{-2}$$
$$= \binom{3}{18}$$
$$\underline{c} = \binom{1}{6} \quad \text{So C is the point } (1, 6).$$

So the smaller circle has equation $(x-1)^2 + (y-6)^2 = (2\sqrt{2})^2 = 8.$

4

See *Trigonometry* §5

$$2\cos2x - 5\cos x - 4 = 0$$
$$2(2\cos^2x - 1) - 5\cos x - 4 = 0$$
$$4\cos^2x - 5\cos x - 6 = 0$$
$$(4\cos x + 3)(\cos x - 2) = 0$$

Using:
$$\cos2A = 2\cos^2A - 1$$

$$\cos x = -\frac{3}{4}$$

or $\cos x = 2$ no solutions

$$a = \cos^{-1}\left(\frac{3}{4}\right) = 0.723 \text{ (to 3 d.p.)}$$

$$x = \pi - 0.723 \quad \text{or} \quad \pi + 0.723$$
$$= 2.419 \quad \text{or} \quad 3.865$$

5

(a) See *Straight Lines* §1
(b) See *Differentiation* §12

a **i** When $x = 0$ on the lower curve, $y = \frac{2}{5}(10 - 0) = 4$. So $T(0,4)$.

Since $TP = x$, the x-coordinate of P is x.

So Q has y-coordinate $y = 10 - x^2$.

P and Q have x-coordinate 4, so PQ is the difference in y-coordinates.

Hence $PQ = 10 - x^2 - 4 = 6 - x^2$ units.

ii The shaded area is $A(x) = 2 \times x \times (6 - x^2) = 12x - 2x^3$.

b Stationary points exist where $A'(x) = 0$.

$$A'(x) = 12 - 6x^2 = 0$$
$$x^2 = 2$$
$$x = \pm\sqrt{2}.$$

Since x is a length (ie not negative) $x = \sqrt{2}$.

When $x = \sqrt{2}$, $A(\sqrt{2}) = 12\sqrt{2} - 2\sqrt{2}^3 = 8\sqrt{2}$.

cont...

2010

Justify nature…

Method 1 Nature table:

x	$\sqrt{2}^-$	$\sqrt{2}$	$\sqrt{2}^+$
$A'(x)$	$+$	0	$-$
Sketch	$/$	$-$	$\searrow$

Method 2 Second derivative test: $A''(x) = -12x$.

When $x = \sqrt{2}$, $A''(\sqrt{2}) = -12\sqrt{2} < 0$.

So the maximum area is $8\sqrt{2}$ square units which occurs when $x = \sqrt{2}$.

6

(a) See **Further Calculus** §3 and §4, and **Differentiation** §5
(c) See **Integration** §5, §6 and §7

a Using the chain rule…

$$\frac{dy}{dx} = \frac{1}{2}(2x-9)^{-1/2} \times \frac{d}{dx}(2x)$$

Remember: $\frac{dy}{dx} = m_{tangent}$

$$= \frac{1}{2} \cdot \frac{1}{\sqrt{2x-9}} \times 2$$

$$= \frac{1}{\sqrt{2x-9}}$$

When $x = 9$, $\frac{dy}{dx} = \frac{1}{\sqrt{9}} = \frac{1}{3}$.

and $y = (18-9)^{1/2} = \sqrt{9} = 3$.

So the equation of the tangent is $y - 3 = \frac{1}{3}(x-9)$

$$3y - 9 = x - 9$$

$$y = \frac{1}{3}x.$$

cont…

2010

b Put $y = 0$ in the equation of the curve...

$$\sqrt{2x - 9} = 0$$
$$2x - 9 = 0$$
$$x = \frac{9}{2}.$$

So A is the point $\left(\frac{9}{2}, 0\right)$.

c Method 1

Calculate the area of the large triangle between $x = 0$ and $x = 9$, then subtract the area under the curve between A and $x = 9$.

The area of the triangle is $\frac{1}{2} \times$ base $\times$ height $= \frac{1}{2} \times 9 \times 3 = \frac{27}{2}$.

The area under the curve is

$$\int_{9/2}^{9} (2x - 9)^{\frac{1}{2}} \, dx = \left[\frac{(2x - 9)^{3/2}}{\frac{3}{2} \times 2} \right]_{9/2}^{9}$$

$$= \left[\frac{1}{3} (2x - 9)^{3/2} \right]_{9/2}^{9}$$

$$= \left(\frac{1}{3} \times 3^3 - 0 \right)$$

$$= 9$$

Remember:
$$\int (ax + b)^n \, dx$$
$$= \frac{(ax + b)^{n+1}}{a(n+1)} + c$$

So the shaded area is $\frac{27}{2} - 9 = \frac{9}{2}$ (or $4\frac{1}{2}$) square units.

cont...

Method 2 Rearrange for x and integrate with respect to y.

Curve: $y = \sqrt{2x-9}$ Line: $y = \frac{1}{3}x$
$\qquad y^2 = 2x - 9$ $x = 3y$.
$\qquad x = \frac{1}{2}(y^2 + 9)$

The shaded area lies between the line and curve and $y = 0$ and $y = 3$, so is given by

$$\int_0^3 (\text{upper} - \text{lower})\, dy = \int_0^3 \left(\frac{1}{2}(y^2 + 9) - 3y\right) dy$$

$$= \int_0^3 \left(\frac{1}{2}y^2 - 3y + \frac{9}{2}\right) dy$$

$$= \left[\frac{1}{6}y^3 - \frac{3}{2}y^2 + \frac{9}{2}y\right]_0^3$$

$$= \frac{1}{6}\times 3^3 - \frac{3}{2}\times 3^2 + \frac{9}{2}\times 3$$

$$= \frac{9}{2} \quad \left(= 4\frac{1}{2}\right)$$

Hence the shaded area is $\frac{9}{2}$ $\left(\text{or } 4\frac{1}{2}\right)$ square units.

---

7   *See **Exponentials and Logarithms** §3*

a $\log_4 x = P$
$\Leftrightarrow \quad 4^P = x$
$\qquad \log_{16} 4^P = \log_{16} x$
$\qquad P . \log_{16} 4 = \log_{16} x$
$\qquad \log_{16} x = \frac{1}{2} P.$ since $\log_{16} 4 = \frac{1}{2}$

> Remember
> $\log_a b$ is the power of a that gives b.

b   Similarly, $\log_3 x = 2\log_9 x$. So the equation becomes

$\qquad 2\log_9 x + \log_9 x = 12$
$\qquad\qquad \log_9 x = 4$
$\qquad\qquad\quad x = 9^4$

> Remember:
> $\log_a x = b \Leftrightarrow x = a^b.$

1

See **Vectors** §5 and §6

$$2p - q - \frac{1}{2}r = 2\begin{pmatrix} 2 \\ 5 \\ -7 \end{pmatrix} - \begin{pmatrix} 1 \\ 0 \\ -1 \end{pmatrix} - \frac{1}{2}\begin{pmatrix} -4 \\ 2 \\ 0 \end{pmatrix}$$

$$= \begin{pmatrix} 4 \\ 10 \\ -14 \end{pmatrix} - \begin{pmatrix} 1 \\ 0 \\ -1 \end{pmatrix} - \begin{pmatrix} -2 \\ 1 \\ 0 \end{pmatrix}$$

$$= \begin{pmatrix} 5 \\ 9 \\ -13 \end{pmatrix}.$$

C

2

See **Straight Lines** §3 and §6

Any line parallel to l has the same gradient.

To extract the gradient, rearrange to give $y = mx + c$ ...

$$3y + 2x = 6$$
$$3y = -2x + 6$$
$$y = -\frac{2}{3}x + 2.$$

So l has gradient $-\frac{2}{3}$.

B

3

See **Functions and Graphs** §10

The graph of $y = f(x+2) - 1$
is $y = f(x)$ shifted
• 2 units to the left and
• 1 unit down.

D

4

See **Differentiation** §5

$$\frac{dy}{dx} = 3x^2 - 2$$

Remember: the derivative gives the gradient of the tangent

When $x = 2$, the gradient of the tangent is $3 \times 2^2 - 2 = 10$.

D

5

See **Polynomials and Quadratics** §3

Method 1 Compensating...

$$x^2 - 8x + 7 = (x-4)^2 - 16 + 7 = (x-4)^2 - 9 \quad . \quad \text{So } q = -9$$

This gives the correct x^2 and x terms, and an extra 16

Take off this extra 16

Method 2 Comparing coefficients...

$$x^2 - 8x + 7 = (x-p)^2 + q$$
$$= x^2 - 2px + p^2 + q .$$

So $-2p = -8$ and $p^2 + q = 7$
$\quad p = 4 \qquad\qquad q = 7 - 16$
$\qquad\qquad\qquad\qquad = -9$

A

6

See **Circles** §6

The tangent is perpendicular to CP so $\quad m_{cp} \times m_{tgt} = -1$;
hence $m_{tgt} = \frac{1}{2}$.

So the equation is $\quad y - (-3) = \frac{1}{2}(x - 2) \quad$ using $P(2, -3)$.

$$y + 3 = \frac{1}{2}(x - 2)$$

C

7

See **Polynomials and Quadratics** §9

The remainder is

$$f(1) = 1^3 - 1^2 + 1 + 3 = 4$$

You could have used synthetic division

D

8

See **Straight Lines** §3 and **Functions and Graphs** §8

$$m = \tan \vartheta = \tan 30° = \frac{1}{\sqrt{3}} .$$

Exact values...

A

9

See **Polynomials and Quadratics** §2

Since $23 > 0$, the equation has real roots. So (1) is correct.

The roots could be rational or irrational, e.g.

- $\frac{1}{2}x^2 + 5x + 1 = 0$ has solutions $x = -5 \pm \sqrt{23}$.
- $\sqrt{23}\,x^2 + \sqrt{23}\,x = 0$ has solutions $x = 0$, $x = -1$.

Hence statement (2) is not true in general.

B

---

10 $2\cos x = \sqrt{3}$

See **Trigonometry** §1

$$\cos x = \frac{\sqrt{3}}{2}$$

$$\begin{array}{c|c} \pi - a & \sqrt{}\ a \\ \hline S & A \\ \hline \pi + a & T\ C\ \checkmark \\ & 2\pi - a \end{array}$$

$$a = \cos^{-1}\left(\frac{\sqrt{3}}{2}\right)$$

$$= \frac{\pi}{6}$$

Exact values...

(triangle with sides 2, $\sqrt{3}$, 1 and angles $\pi/6$, $\pi/3$)

So $x = \dfrac{\pi}{6}$ or $2\pi - \dfrac{\pi}{6} = \dfrac{11\pi}{6}$

D

11

See **Integration** §1

$$\int \left(4x^{1/2} + x^{-3}\right)dx = \frac{4x^{3/2}}{3/2} + \frac{x^{-2}}{-2} + C = \frac{8}{3}x^{3/2} - \frac{1}{2}x^{-2} + c.$$

D

12

See **Trigonometry** §3

$$\sin(p+q) = \sin p \cos q + \cos p \sin q$$

Using the formulae list

From the diagram,

$$\sin p = \frac{opp.}{hyp.} = \frac{2}{\sqrt{5}}, \quad \cos p = \frac{adj.}{hyp.} = \frac{1}{\sqrt{5}},$$

$$\sin q = \frac{2}{3} \quad \text{and} \quad \cos q = \frac{\sqrt{5}}{3}.$$

So $\sin(p+q) = \dfrac{2}{\sqrt{5}} \times \dfrac{\sqrt{5}}{3} + \dfrac{1}{\sqrt{5}} \times \dfrac{2}{3} = \dfrac{2}{3} + \dfrac{2}{3\sqrt{5}}.$

C

2011

13

See **Further Calculus** §1

$f(x) = 4\sin 3x$

$f'(x) = 4 \times 3\cos 3x$
$\qquad = 12\cos 3x$

$\left\{ \text{Using: } \dfrac{d}{dx}\left(\sin ax\right) = a\cos ax \right\}$

So $f'(0) = 12\cos(0) = 12$.

C

14

See **Vectors** §11

Since the triangle is equilateral, the angle θ between $\underline{p}$ and $\underline{q}$ is 60°.

$\underline{p} \cdot \underline{q} = |\underline{p}||\underline{q}|\cos\theta$
$\qquad = 3 \times 3 \times \cos 60°$
$\qquad = 9 \times \dfrac{1}{2}$
$\qquad = \dfrac{9}{2}$.

Exact values...

2, 30°, $\sqrt{3}$, 60°, 1

B

15

See **Vectors** §10

$\overrightarrow{ST} = \underline{t} - \underline{s} = \begin{pmatrix} -16 \\ -4 \\ 16 \end{pmatrix} - \begin{pmatrix} -4 \\ 5 \\ 1 \end{pmatrix} = \begin{pmatrix} -12 \\ -9 \\ 15 \end{pmatrix} = -3\begin{pmatrix} 4 \\ 3 \\ -5 \end{pmatrix}$

$\overrightarrow{TU} = \underline{u} - \underline{t} = \begin{pmatrix} -24 \\ -10 \\ 26 \end{pmatrix} - \begin{pmatrix} -16 \\ -4 \\ 16 \end{pmatrix} = \begin{pmatrix} -8 \\ -6 \\ 10 \end{pmatrix} = -2\begin{pmatrix} 4 \\ 3 \\ -5 \end{pmatrix} = \dfrac{2}{3}\overrightarrow{ST}$

So $\dfrac{ST}{TU} = \dfrac{3}{2}$, i.e. T divides SU in the ratio $3:2$.

B

16

See **Integration** §1 and §2

$\displaystyle\int \dfrac{1}{3x^4}\,dx = \dfrac{1}{3}\int x^{-4}\,dx = \dfrac{1}{3} \times \dfrac{x^{-3}}{-3} + c = -\dfrac{1}{9x^3} + c.$

A

17

See **Polynomials and Quadratics** §12

The cubic crosses the x-axis at $x=-1$, $x=0$ and $x=2$; so its equation is

$$y = k\left(x-(-1)\right)x\left(x-2\right) = kx(x+1)(x-2)$$

for some constant k.

When $x=1$, $y=2$ so $2= k \times 1 \times 2 \times (-1)$ i.e. $k=-1$. **A**

18

See **Polynomials and Quadratics** §6

The graph is above the x-axis when

$$(x-3)(x+5)>0.$$

From the sketch, $x<-5$ or $x>3$.

Sketch:

$y=(x-3)(x+5)$

C

19

See **Exponentials and Logarithms** §2 and **Functions and Graphs** §5

When $x=1$, $\log_3 y = 1$ i.e. $y=3^1=3$

When $x=0$, $\log_3 y = 0$ i.e. $y=3^0=1$.

Remember:
$x = \log_a y \Leftrightarrow y = a^x$.

So the curve passes through $(1,3)$ and $(0,1)$ **C**

20

See **Functions and Graphs** §2, §3 and §9

$$g(x) = \sin^2\sqrt{x-2}.$$

Since we are taking the square root of $x-2$, we need

$$x-2 \geqslant 0 \quad \text{i.e.} \quad x \geqslant 2.$$

Since $\sqrt{x-2}$ can have any value $\geqslant 0$, $-1 \leqslant \sin\sqrt{x-2} \leqslant 1$.

Hence $0 \leqslant g(x) \leqslant 1$. **D**

2011

21

See **Straight Lines** – (a) §6, (b) §10, (c) §9 and §6

a

$$m_{BD} = \frac{-3-12}{2-7} = \frac{-15}{-5} = 3.$$

So the equation of BD is $\quad y-(-3) = 3(x-2) \quad$ using $D(2,-3)$.

$$y+3 = 3x-6$$
$$3x-y-9 = 0.$$

b Solve the equations of BD and AC simultaneously...

$$3x - y = 9 \quad ---\,①$$
$$x + 3y = 23 \quad ---\,②$$

$3 \times ① + ② : \quad 10x = 50$
$$x = 5$$

Put $x=5$ into $①$: $y = 3\times5 - 9 = 6$. So E is the point $(5,6)$.

c i

$$m_{AB} = \frac{12-8}{7+1} = \frac{4}{8} = \frac{1}{2}. \quad \text{So } m_\perp = -2 \text{ since } m_{AB} \times m_\perp = -1.$$

$$\text{midpoint}_{AB} = \left(\frac{-1+7}{2}, \frac{8+12}{2} \right) = (3,10).$$

Then the equation of the perpendicular bisector is

$$y - 10 = -2(x-3)$$
$$y - 10 = -2x + 6$$
$$y + 2x - 16 = 0. \quad ---\, (*)$$

ii Put $x=5$ and $y=6$ in the left-hand side of $(*)$ and check we get the right-hand side...

$$6 + 2\times5 - 16 = 0.$$

So the line passes through E.

22

(a) See **Differentiation** §9
(b) See **Differentiation** §7 and §8
(c) See **Functions and Graphs** §10

a **i** The curve cuts the x-axis when $y=0$ i.e.

$$(x-2)(x^2+1) = 0$$
$$x = 2 \quad \text{or} \quad x^2 = -1 \leftarrow \text{no real solutions}$$

So the curve cuts the x-axis at $(2,0)$.

ii The curve cuts the y-axis when $x=0$ i.e.

$$y = (0-2)(0^2+1) = -2.$$

So the curve cuts the y-axis at $(0,-2)$.

b Stationary points exist where $f'(x) = 0$.

$$f(x) = (x-2)(x^2+1) = x^3 - 2x^2 + x - 2$$
$$f'(x) = 3x^2 - 4x + 1 = 0$$
$$(3x-1)(x-1) = 0.$$
$$x = \frac{1}{3} \quad \text{and} \quad x = 1.$$

When $x = \frac{1}{3}$, $\quad y = \left(\frac{1}{3} - 2\right)\left(\left(\frac{1}{3}\right)^2 + 1\right) = -\frac{5}{3} \times \frac{10}{9} = -\frac{50}{27}$.

When $x = 1$, $\quad y = (1-2)(1^2+1) = -2$.

So the stationary points are $\left(\frac{1}{3}, -\frac{50}{27}\right)$ and $(1,-2)$.

Justify nature...

Method 1 Nature table:

x	$\frac{1}{3}^-$	$\frac{1}{3}$	$\frac{1}{3}^+$	1^-	1	1^+
$f'(x)$	$+$	0	$-$	$+$	0	$-$
Sketch	/	—	\	\	—	/

Method 2 Second derivative test: $f''(x) = 6x - 4$

When $x = \frac{1}{3}$, $f''\left(\frac{1}{3}\right) = 6 \times \frac{1}{3} - 4 = -2 < 0$.

When $x = 1$, $f''(1) = 6 \times 1 - 4 = 2 > 0$

So $\left(\frac{1}{3}, -\frac{50}{27}\right)$ is a maximum turning point

$(1,-2)$ is a minimum turning point.

cont...

2011

c **i**

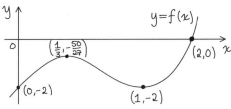

ii For the graph of $y = -f(x)$, reflect in the x-axis.

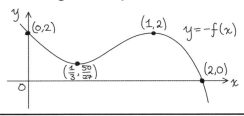

23

See **Trigonometry** §4 and §5

a
$$\cos 2x° - 3\cos x° + 2 = 0$$
$$2\cos^2 x° - 1 - 3\cos x° + 2 = 0$$
$$2\cos^2 x° - 3\cos x° + 1 = 0$$
$$(2\cos x° - 1)(\cos x° - 1) = 0.$$

Using:
$$\cos 2A = 2\cos^2 A - 1$$

$2\cos x° - 1 = 0$
$\cos x° = \dfrac{1}{2}$

	a
180 - a	S A ✓
	T C ✓
180 + a	360 - a

$a = \cos^{-1}\left(\dfrac{1}{2}\right)$
$= 60$

or

Exact values...

[right triangle with sides 2, $\sqrt{3}$, 1 and angles 30°, 60°]

$\cos x° - 1 = 0$
$\cos x° = 1$
$x = 0$

$x = 60$ or $360 - 60$

So $x = 0, 60$ or 300

b Let $u = 2x$, then the equation becomes
$$\cos 2u° - 3\cos u° + 2 = 0.$$

Since $0 \le x < 360,\ 0 \le u < 720.$

From part (a), $u = 0, 60, 300, 360, 420, 660, ~~720~~$

So $x = 0, 30, 150, \underline{180}, 210, 330.$

↳ too big

1

*See **Vectors** – (a) §2 and §5, (b) §7, and (c) §12*

a $B(4,4,0)$ since OABC is a square with side length 4.

b $\overrightarrow{DB} = \underline{b} - \underline{d} = \begin{pmatrix} 4 \\ 4 \\ 0 \end{pmatrix} - \begin{pmatrix} 2 \\ 2 \\ 6 \end{pmatrix} = \begin{pmatrix} 2 \\ 2 \\ -6 \end{pmatrix}$

M lies half-way along OA, so M is $(2,0,0)$.

$$\overrightarrow{DM} = \underline{m} - \underline{d} = \begin{pmatrix} 2 \\ 0 \\ 0 \end{pmatrix} - \begin{pmatrix} 2 \\ 2 \\ 6 \end{pmatrix} = \begin{pmatrix} 0 \\ -2 \\ -6 \end{pmatrix}$$

c $B\hat{D}M$ is the angle between $\overrightarrow{DB}$ and $\overrightarrow{DM}$

$$|\overrightarrow{DB}| = \sqrt{2^2 + 2^2 + (-6)^2} = \sqrt{44} = 2\sqrt{11}$$
$$|\overrightarrow{DM}| = \sqrt{0^2 + (-2)^2 + (-6)^2} = \sqrt{40} = 2\sqrt{10}$$

Method 1 $\quad \cos B\hat{D}M = \dfrac{\overrightarrow{DB} \cdot \overrightarrow{DM}}{|\overrightarrow{DB}||\overrightarrow{DM}|}$

Using: $\underline{a} \cdot \underline{b} = |\underline{a}||\underline{b}|\cos\vartheta$

$$= \frac{2 \times 0 + 2 \times (-2) + (-6) \times (-6)}{4\sqrt{10}\sqrt{11}}$$

$$= \frac{8}{\sqrt{10}\sqrt{11}}$$

$$B\hat{D}M = \cos^{-1}\left(\frac{8}{\sqrt{10}\sqrt{11}}\right)$$
$$= 40 \cdot 29° \text{ (to 2 d.p.)}$$
$$\text{OR } 0 \cdot 703 \text{ rads (to 3 d.p.)}$$

cont...

Method 2 $|\overrightarrow{MB}| = \left|\begin{pmatrix} 2 \\ 4 \\ 0 \end{pmatrix}\right| = \sqrt{4+16} = \sqrt{20} = 2\sqrt{5}$

$\cos B\hat{D}M = \dfrac{44+40-20}{8\sqrt{10}\sqrt{11}}$

$= \dfrac{8}{\sqrt{10}\sqrt{11}}$

Remember the cosine rule:

$\cos A = \dfrac{b^2+c^2-a^2}{2bc}$

So $B\hat{D}M = 40.29°$ (to 2 d.p.) or 0.703 rads (to 3 d.p.)

2

*(a) and (b) See **Functions and Graphs** §3*
*(c) and (d) See **Polynomials and Quadratics** §9*

a $g(f(x)) = g(x^3-1) = 3(x^3-1)+1 = 3x^3-2$

b $g(f(x)) + xh(x) = 3x^3-2 + x(4x-5)$
$= 3x^3-2+4x^2-5x$
$= 3x^3+4x^2-5x-2.$

c i $x-1$ is a factor $\Leftrightarrow$ the expression is zero when $x=1$.

Method 1 When $x=1$, $3(1)^3+4(1)^2-5(1)-2 = 0$

Method 2 Using synthetic division...

$$
\begin{array}{r|rrrr}
1 & 3 & 4 & -5 & -2 \\
  &   & 3 & 7 & 2 \\
\hline
  & 3 & 7 & 2 & \boxed{0}
\end{array}
$$

Since the expression is zero, $x-1$ is a factor.

ii $3x^3+4x^2-5x-2 = (x-1)(3x^2+7x-2)$ ← By inspection or from the table.
$= (x-1)(3x+1)(x+2)$

d $g(f(x)) + xh(x) = 0$
$(x-1)(3x+1)(x+2) = 0$
$x = 1$ or $x = -\dfrac{1}{3}$ or $x = -2.$

3

See **Sequences** – (a) §2, (b) §5, (c) §4

a

$u_0 = -16$

$u_1 = -\frac{1}{2} u_0 = -\frac{1}{2} \times (-16) = 8$

$u_2 = -\frac{1}{2} \times u_1 = -\frac{1}{2} \times 8 = -4$

b We know that $v_2 = 5$ and $v_3 = 7$, so $5 = 4p + q$ and $7 = 5p + q$.

Solving simultaneously...

$5 = 4p + q$ ———— ①
$7 = 5p + q$ ———— ②

②-①: $p = 2$.

When $p = 2$, $q = 5 - 4 \times 2 = -3$.

c **i** Since $-1 < -\frac{1}{2} < 1$, the sequence in (a) has a limit.

Method 1 $l = \frac{b}{1-a}$ with $a = -\frac{1}{2}$ and $b = 0$.

So $l = 0$.

Method 2 As $n \to \infty$, $u_{n+1} = u_n = l$

So $l = -\frac{1}{2} l$

$\frac{3}{2} l = 0$

$l = 0$

ii The sequence from (b) does not have a limit since $p = 2 > 1$.

4

See *Integration* §6

The shaded area between $x = -2$ and $x = 0$ is given by

$$\int_{-2}^{0} \left(\text{upper} - \text{lower}\right) dx = \int_{-2}^{0} \left(x^3 - x^2 - 4x + 4 - (2x + 4)\right) dx$$

$$= \int_{-2}^{0} \left(x^3 - x^2 - 6x\right) dx$$

Remember:
$$\int (ax + b)^n dx$$
$$= \frac{(ax + b)^{n+1}}{a(n+1)} + c$$

$$= \left[\frac{1}{4} x^4 - \frac{1}{3} x^3 - 3x^2\right]_{-2}^{0}$$

$$= 0 - \left(\frac{1}{4}(-2)^4 - \frac{1}{3}(-2)^3 - 3(-2)^2\right)$$

$$= -\frac{16}{4} - \frac{8}{3} + 12$$

$$= 8 - \frac{8}{3}$$

$$= \frac{16}{3}$$

The shaded area between $x = 0$ and $x = 3$ is given by

$$\int_{0}^{3} \left(\text{upper} - \text{lower}\right) dx = \int_{0}^{3} \left(2x + 4 - (x^3 - x^2 - 4x + 4)\right) dx$$

$$= \int_{0}^{3} \left(-x^3 + x^2 + 6x\right) dx$$

$$= \left[-\frac{1}{4} x^4 + \frac{1}{3} x^3 + 3x^2\right]_{0}^{3}$$

$$= -\frac{1}{4} \times 3^4 + \frac{1}{3} \times 3^3 + 3 \times 3^2 - 0$$

$$= -\frac{81}{4} + 9 + 27$$

$$= \frac{63}{4}$$

So the shaded area is $\frac{16}{3} + \frac{63}{4} = \frac{253}{12}$ $\left(\text{or } 21\frac{1}{12}\right)$ square units.

5

See **Exponentials and Logarithms** §6

We are told $y = kx^n$. Taking $\log_2$ gives

$$\log_2 y = \log_2 (kx^n)$$
$$= \log_2 k + \log_2 x^n$$
$$= \log_2 k + n\log_2 x$$
$$= n\log_2 x + \log_2 k.$$

The line has gradient $\dfrac{7-5}{4-0} = \dfrac{1}{2}$, so $n = \dfrac{1}{2}$.

The line passes through $(0,5)$, so $\log_2 k = 5$ i.e. $k = 2^5 = 32$.

6

(a) See **Wave Functions** §1 and §2
(b) See **Further Calculus** §2 and **Trigonometry** §5

a

$$3\sin x - 5\cos x = R\sin(x+a)$$
$$= R\sin x \cos a + R\cos x \sin a$$
$$= (R\cos a)\sin x + (R\sin a)\cos x$$

Comparing coefficients: $\quad R\cos a = 3$
$\qquad\qquad\qquad\qquad\quad R\sin a = -5$

So $R = \sqrt{3^2 + (-5)^2}$ and $\tan a = -\dfrac{5}{3}$
$\quad = \sqrt{34}$
$\qquad\qquad\qquad\qquad\qquad a = 2\pi - \tan^{-1}\left(\dfrac{5}{3}\right)$
$\qquad\qquad\qquad\qquad\qquad\quad = 5.253 \text{ (to 3 d.p.)}$

So $3\sin x - 5\cos x = \sqrt{34}\sin(x + 5.253)$.

cont...

2011

b

$$\int_0^t (3\cos x + 5\sin x)\, dx = \left[3\sin x - 5\cos x \right]_0^t$$
$$= 3\sin t - 5\cos t - (3\sin 0 - 5\cos 0)$$
$$= 3\sin t - 5\cos t + 5.$$

So the equation becomes
$$3\sin t - 5\cos t + 5 = 3$$
$$\sqrt{34}\,\sin(t + 5\cdot 253) = -2$$
$$\sin(t + 5\cdot 253) = -\frac{2}{\sqrt{34}}$$

$$\begin{array}{c|c}
\pi - a & a \\
S & A \\
\hline
\sqrt{T} & C \sqrt{} \\
\pi + a & 2\pi - a
\end{array}$$

$$a = \sin^{-1}\left(\frac{2}{\sqrt{34}}\right)$$
$$= 0\cdot 350 \ (\text{to } 3\,\text{d.p.})$$

$$\begin{array}{lll}
t + 5\cdot 253 = \pi + 0\cdot 350 & \text{or} & 2\pi - 0\cdot 350 \\
t = -1\cdot 761 & \text{or} & 0\cdot 680.
\end{array}$$

Since $0 \leq t \leq 2$, the solution is $t = 0\cdot 68$ (to 2 d.p.).

7

See **Circles** §1, §3 and §7

Circle C_1 has centre $(-1, 1)$ and radius $r_1 = \sqrt{121} = 11$

Circle C_2 has centre $(2, -3)$ and radius $r_2 = \sqrt{2^2 + (-3)^2 + p} = \sqrt{13 - p}$

The distance between the centres is
$$d = \sqrt{(-3-1)^2 + (2+1)^2}$$
$$= \sqrt{25}$$
$$= 5.$$

Since the circles do not touch,
$$5 + r_2 < r_1 \ \text{i.e.}$$

$$5 + \sqrt{13 - p} < 11$$
$$\sqrt{13 - p} < 6$$
$$13 - p < 36$$
$$p > -23.$$

> The circle
> $(x-a)^2 + (y-b)^2 = r^2$
> has centre (a, b) and radius r.

> The circle
> $x^2 + y^2 + 2gx + 2fy + c = 0$
> has centre $(-g, -f)$ and radius $\sqrt{g^2 + f^2 - c}$

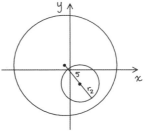

In addition we need $13 - p > 0$, since $r_2 = \sqrt{13 - p}$, ie $p < 13$.
Hence $-23 < p < 13$.